Kari Caldwell's
LITTLE BOOK OF ENERGY

 SIX STRATEGIES

To Leverage Negativity

&

Create Everyday Miracles

Kari Caldwell

Little Book of Energy

The Energy Positive Perspective and Six Strategies to Leverage Negativity and Create Everyday Miracles

By Kari Caldwell

Copyright © 2015 by Kari Caldwell

All rights reserved. No part of this book may be reproduced in any form or by any electronic or mechanical means, including information storage and retrieval systems, without permission in writing from the publisher. For information, contact Kari Caldwell, at www.energypositivelife.com.

Author's Note: The content of this book is for general instruction only. The ideas and suggestions contained within this book are not intended to replace consultation with licensed physicians or counselors. The author and publisher are not rendering professional advice or services and are not responsible for any and all health or medical needs. Please consult a physician if you require medical attention and/or supervision. The author and publisher are not liable or responsible for loss or damage allegedly arising from suggestion or information in this book.

Printed in the United States of America

ISBN: 0692561935

ISBN-13: 978-0692561935

Copyright © 2015 Kari Caldwell

All rights reserved.

DEDICATION

*To Owen, Lincoln, Dylan
And Brandon*

You fill my heart with an abundance of love, light and laughter. May these energies always guide you, and give you the freedom to see the miracles that you are.

And

*To my Mom,
Your dedication and love have given me the strength and courage to step outside my comfort zones, find my wings and soar. Thank you.*

INTENTION

It is my deepest desire that this book reveal the perspective needed to miraculously transform the negativity in your life, and give you strength and vision to attract positive, expansive energies.

LITTLE BOOK OF ENERGY

TABLE OF CONTENTS

Prologue	XI
Introduction	XV
Energy Positive+ Defined	XXVI
Observing Energy: Your New Blood Type E+	XXIV

PART I

The Energy Positive Perspective

1	Everything Is Energy	37
2	Infinite Possibilities	41
3	Energy Expands and Contracts	47
4	Everything Radiates a Unique Energetic Signature	51
5	Energy Lives Within Us: Emotions and Thoughts	57
6	Energy is Constantly Communicating	65
7	Energy is Constantly Transforming	69

TABLE OF CONTENTS

PART II

STRATEGIES: CREATING AN ENERGY POSITIVE+ LIFE

STRATEGY ONE: CHANGE YOUR CHOICE	89
STRATEGY TWO: DREAM BIG	107
STRATEGY THREE: OWN YOUR STORY	125
STRATEGY FOUR: FUEL YOUR ENERGY BODY	149
STRATEGY FIVE: PRACTICE, PRACTICE, PRACTICE	167
STRATEGY SIX: EXPECT MIRACLES	187

TABLE OF CONTENTS

PART III

THE ENERGY POSITIVE+ LIFESTYLE

ENERGY POSITIVE+ GUIDELINES	221
STRATEGY 1: RECLAIMING POWER	227
STRATEGY 2: INTENTION SETTING	229
STRATEGY 3: RELEASING	237
STRATEGY 4: REGENERATIVE ENERGY	243
STRATEGY 5: ACHIEVING BALANCE & SYNCHRONICITY	255
STRATEGY 6: GRATITUDE AND RECEIVING	267

Kari Caldwell

DEAL FROM STRENGTH.

-EDWARD KAMM

Kari Caldwell

Prologue

When was the last time someone told you to "Just think positive thoughts"? Most likely it was at a difficult or poignant moment when you needed help, sympathy, or empathy. Did the advice help? Make you feel better? Most likely, just thinking positive thoughts doesn't get you out of a terrible situation or change your life. What CAN you do when experiencing misery, pain, or grief to pull yourself together, and feel hopeful and positive and enthusiastic again?

I've always been a relatively optimistic individual, but in those moments when my stress is peaked, or my sorrow seems agonizing, or my anger is supreme, considering a shift to adopting a positive, alternative perspective seems a very great challenge. I'd often rather simply continue to wallow in my misery and feel depressed and angry or that I can't accomplish anything. As a young adult I was not personally acquainted with the "self-help" and positive-thought reading material. But as the pressure mounted with the arrival of three boys in four years, and I experienced a downturn in the economy, I began to recognize that whatever coping mechanisms I had attained thus far were, plain and simple, not working. To say I felt overwhelmed is a great understatement! I wanted to feel carefree and joyous, but found many days were filled with stress that I couldn't control. With the kids growing, I needed to change as much for them as for myself.

My brother, the ever-motivated, self-help junkie, offered his assistance by loading me up with books by Tony Robbins and Jack Canfield among other great thinkers. These sources were supposed to have the key to my future happiness and success. But no matter how hard I tried or how many vision boards I created, I could not seem to get any of my improvement efforts to stick. I was clearly missing an ingredient in the magical success formula that everyone around me seemed to have found. And while I maintained an optimistic perspective in my search for answers, my daily thoughts were beginning to take on a tone of desperation.

It felt at times like I had brewed a perfect storm. But at some time in the midst of my whirl, I experienced a few key random conversations with friends that included a series of seemingly unrelated ideas. And, one of these centered on an unnaturally piqued interest in quantum physics. Ultimately, all the ideas together collided in an unexpected, perfectly synchronistic awareness that would forever shift how I understood my life.

Initially, I couldn't see the profound impact of watching shows like "Through the Wormhole" with Morgan Freeman, yet I couldn't seem to get enough of them. As I pieced all of these clues together, a relationship between physics and the human body began to capture my imagination, and a far grander ingredient to a successful life than just positive thought began to present itself.

As I experienced a keener awareness of the inner-workings and role of my thoughts, emotions and beliefs, I saw how they played in my body physically and how they impacted my experiences. Eventually, a pattern emerged—a new perspective began to unveil itself. I began to recognize the relationship between my thoughts and beliefs and my ability to fluently speak this energetic language.

It became evident that spending time focusing on symptoms (such as frequent migraines or stress over forgone opportunities), instead of on underlying perspectives, had limited my ability to move beyond my circumstances, and was directly influencing and limiting my destiny.

In the years following this amazing awareness, I dedicated myself to understanding this wondrous and mysterious thought process, and what it meant to attempt to use and follow it in my life. As I explored this new approach to reasoning, my thoughts took on a new tone; and I also began to notice changes in my body and how I interacted with my environment. My senses became more heightened; my enjoyment and appreciation of other people increased. Physically, my lifelong struggle with migraines came to a miraculous halt.

The more I applied this new perspective, the more I recognized even greater concepts, rules and guidelines that gave shape and structure to my life. This structure that is based on scientific evidence was important to my analytical mind, since I needed factual information to sustain my belief in this phenomena.

As I gathered my facts, I began to view myself as not just a "physical" being, but a highly complex and dynamic "energetic" being. A new energetic perspective of my body and life presented itself. I saw abundance and infinite wisdom influencing my thoughts and unlocking inherent powers within my body, mind, and soul. I saw a language of the universe being spoken within me.

Introduction

THE PROVERBIAL TOOLBOX

When we hear the word, toolbox, we might quickly think of a physical box that contains tools to solve problems. We know that the pliers, hammer, wrench, or screw driver are readily available to fix items that are physically broken. Not all of us even own such a toolbox; we may simply borrow tools when we need them.

In this book you will learn about another kind of toolbox that exists; and this particular one each of us not only has in our possession, but we readily and frequently use. The question is: How well stocked is this personal toolbox? Does it meet your needs? Are the tools in it the ones that are the best to solve the problems you encounter? This very special, proverbial toolbox is a part of our very being, and contains valuable insight, strategies, methodology, and coping mechanisms for our survival and success in everyday life.

Depending on our beliefs, culture, and experience, our toolbox likely includes a blend of religious doctrine, family concepts, and varied thought perspectives. We build and fill our proverbial toolbox over our lives through our abilities to observe and learn. All of us cheer on the successful athlete, coach, business executive, mom, or entrepreneur, and then attempt to replicate their formulas—from their toolboxes—and adapt them to our own use, thus adding to our own arsenal of coping strategies.

Think about it.

What observations do you generally make? What lessons have you learned? And what tools are in your proverbial toolbox as a result? Do you use them? And most important, how effective are these tools, strategies, or assets you have collected and honed?

A good measure of the quality of your toolbox is how you would rate your success:

In 1956, Earl Nightingale, the forefather of self-improvement, defined success as the progressive realization of worthy goals. But success can also be recognized in the form of good health, material wealth, happiness, or freedom of thought.

How successful are you? And what does success even mean? Are there things in your life that you would like to change? Are you good at adapting your behavior? At emulating others? At figuring out a system to improve your health and wellness? At determining your own independent path through life?

These are just some of the questions you will find answers in the <u>Little Book of Energy</u>. It may also provide insight into why previous attempts to make desired changes were not lasting. The ideas introduced here are dynamic and life-changing: they are guaranteed to spur your imagination so that reaching goals beyond your dreams are within your grasp.

THE MISSING LINK

Why is it that despite our best efforts to be well equipped, have well-adjusted perspectives, and use rational, logical strategies, we still experience failure?

What I've found is that while most empowerment information focuses on the tools for change and offers many interesting, helpful perspectives, the point from which these perspectives are observed fails to recognize the underlying dynamics that make the self-help tools effective. The mechanics that actually transform a situation from a state of negativity to one of general positivity are highly complex. Consequently, you may find yourself well-armed with guidance and tools on such topics as thinking positive thoughts, changing lifestyle eating, or any other various methods for transformation; but you will be lacking clarification on what to do with the certain negative aspects of life that inherently form the basis for our problems.

Feelings of negativity stem from thoughts, events, circumstances, beliefs or emotions that are incongruent with a positive perspective on which joy and happiness are based. The issue, then, is how do we transform our negative thought patterns, where we feel restriction, low or bad energy, sadness, and loss of hope into opposite feelings of worthiness, abundance, joy, and hopefulness? For example, when our world, either suddenly or over time, appears to us as "upside down," how do we "right" it? How do we shift to a positive thought perspective so we can see and truly feel warmth, joy and happiness? What can we change to climb out of our personal abyss? And to feel that our life is "successful"? The answers needed to make this profound personal transformation are found simply by adjusting our point of observation.

THE NATURE OF OBSERVATION

Before we concentrate on fine-tuning our point of observation, let's review a bit about the human process of observing.

Think about your own observations: we mentioned earlier that it's natural to admire others who exude confidence and success, like an accomplished business person, pro athlete, or happy family, and then attempt to replicate the "successful" formula used by those individuals. But, is success this simple? Does this method of observation always work? The answer is all too obvious: No! Let's try to understand why.

The very nature of the human being is to observe. From birth we observe how to best, and most expediently, meet our needs. The need for observation stems from the distinct inability to survive on our own. Unlike other mammals, we cannot walk at birth; we cannot even crawl to find our first source of nourishment. Instead, from the moment we take our first breath, we begin a process of communicating needs and receiving support. This unique communication dance facilitates development of one of our greatest skills: the ability to learn through observation. So, if the missing link is the point from which we are observing, then what are we presently observing? What are we truly seeing?

THE PRESENT OBSERVATION: THE PHYSICAL WORLD AND "IF, THEN"

Through these early interactions, we become conditioned to observe life in fixed and linear terms. Everything from biochemical reactions in our body (such as I am hurt; I need to cry for attention) to understanding the force of gravity (the apple is ripe, so it will fall to the ground) is subject to linear timelines and sequences of events that are supposedly generated through assembly-line-type processes, where information flows directly from point A to B to C.

This <u>linear</u> model of observation is based on the concept that no matter where a problem is evidenced--whether in our body, in our lives, or in the environment—it can be repaired by identifying a specific infraction point or reason for malfunction. And, once such a faulty link is restored, there is an immediate expectation of resumed working order. Our observations in life have always supported this linear notion: from the infant cry for food, to dark clouds bringing rain, to a cracked pipe leaking its contents. Our observations of this physical world provide us with predictable, cause and effect results. We calculate mathematical probabilities and astrological phenomena accordingly. All of our modern knowledge is based on observations of our linear and physical world.

THE FIRST TRANSFORMATIONAL STEP

As we have inferred, simply observing in linear fashion a series of actions, does not always bring transformation into our own beings. Watching someone else win a gold medal, build a business, grow a family, or heal from cancer does not mean we are automatically equipped to do the same. If the key to bringing about OUR changes is adjusting our observations, what is such an adjustment?

Quantum physics tells us that the needed adjustment is from perceiving only a physical world to profoundly recognizing an energetic world. At the most fundamental level our universe is completely energetic. This means that every action we've ever seen and every skill we've ever developed comes from an infinite field of energy.

Perceiving things energetically means that every observation of our life is not only physical and linear in nature, but it is also comprised of an unseen, non-linear field of energy that is intelligent and infinitely connected to everything. This intelligent field of energy is capable of organizing, creating, and orchestrating all of the information that we experience in the physical world.

On occasion we recognize and observe this non-linear, inexplicable field for what it is. We might refer to it as our "sixth" sense. We may witness its miraculous nature in the form of a coincidence or irony; but when we witness it firsthand, the experience evokes a profound weirdness, beauty and complexity.

Observing this energetic world and incorporating its lessons with our linear observations is paramount to achieving ultimate transformation. It is precisely this non-linear observation of energy--working with its interconnected layers--that provides us with the missing links; those perspectives and tools we need to effectively manage the "negativity" in our lives.

Little Book

Of

Energy

<u>Little Book of Energy</u> will help fine tune what you actually see and perceive in order to recognize and mitigate the effects of "negativity," "restriction," and "contraction" in your life. We will work to moderate these forces to effect positive transformation–with expansion and fulfillment--on a lifelong basis. In other words, you will learn a variety of skills to ensure your life is positively expanding so your perceptions of unsuccessfulness transform into ones of accomplishment and feeling enriched.

The New Observation:

YOUR NEW BLOOD TYPE: e+ = ENERGY POSITIVE

When we recognize and identify energetic aspects in relation to our body, interactions, and environment, we use a particular perspective; we will refer to this new point of observation as the E+ or Energy Positive perspective. Our ability to observe our own human bio-organism from an energetic perspective--or "Energy Positive" perspective--empowers us to improve or transform our own personal environment, interactions, and choices by revealing the underlying dynamics, and how to engage the inherent "intelligence" within them.

Although you may want to actually "see" the energies contained within our bodies, it is virtually impossible; however, you are able to identify with their physical side effects. Here's an example about feeling the presence of "energy" in your life without actually visualizing it:

Consider your blood type. There is a well-known diet called, "The Blood Type Diet," which maintains, among other things, that you should eat according to what kind of blood type you have. The theory is that different types may have better health or wellness by eating more or less of certain foods. For example, Type As should not eat red meat. In this circumstance, the Type A individual cannot "see" or discriminate without laboratory testing that his or her blood is any different from other blood types. Yet, Type A individuals report feeling substantially better when they follow this "no red meat" protocol. Despite not seeing or feeling like a "Type A," they still recognize improved health and weight loss when implementing the Blood Type Diet protocol.

Similarly, when focusing on identifying the "Energy Positive" perspective, you may find that even though you don't see the effects, you still inherently "know" much of the information you're learning, and can observe or recognize proof of the energy in a specific situation; and you will "see" or recognize proof of the energy in the physical world.

WARNING: These concepts are dense, complex, and occasionally mind-bending, so don't let your "brain go numb"!

The New Observation Defined:

THE ENERGY POSITIVE+ PERSPECTIVE:

The ability to observe our own human bio-organism from both a physical and energetic point of view in order to improve or transform our own personal environment, interactions, and choices by revealing the underlying dynamics and how to engage the inherent "intelligence."

THE ENERGY POSITIVE+ LIFE:

A state of being where expansive and regenerative energies within your awareness are greater than their respective counterparts.

PART ONE

The Energy Positive Perspective

Kari Caldwell

Energy flows where the attention goes.

-Unknown

PART I

THE ENERGY POSITIVE PERSPECTIVE

We all can recall a brief moment in life where something impossible becomes reality. Have you ever wondered how your mind can be thinking a thought, and then the action pictured actually occurs? Have you ever walked into a room and intuitively known which person to approach and which one to avoid? Sometimes everyone in a room can experience an emotion at the same time you do. Sometimes your mind creates an intention and your body then responds. How does your body inherently know how to respond to and process food? All of these experiences are energy at work.

One of the outstanding memories I have of an impossible coincidence was the moment my first son was born. Of course, why wouldn't I remember this momentous event? It occurred in the early hours of the morning, after a long night of laboring in the midst of a hurricane. The impossible coincidence, however, was that my mom, who was two time zones away and in a dead sleep, awakened to the sound of a baby crying. She called my husband's phone before the doctor even handed him our seconds-old newborn. How did she know this? How did she hear him?

I've since experienced many more strange coincidences, from dreams about real life events that occur at a later point in time, to knowing events would occur before they actually do. I've always experienced an intrinsic sense about people, their emotions, and how they can solve situations or create healing for themselves.

Whether extreme moments like mine or more common ones (like "déjà vu"), we all know those flashes that stand still in time or that are too good—and too impossible--to be anything short of a miracle. Our body is naturally designed to speak this energetic language of the universe; accordingly, it can heal and perform functions that are governed beyond the scope of our mind. Unfortunately, we live in a world that systematically interferes with our natural ability to heal and speak this energetic language.

From the mass-produced food we eat, to electromagnetic energy, cell phones, and the barrage of information on the internet and media, we are constantly being assaulted by outside, energetic influences. In addition, our mind is partially responsible for this negative energy. Tasked with the responsibility of ensuring our survival, our mind conjures patterns of behavior, all in the interest of safety and security. While these patterns serve as filters for protection from our environment, they can also distract our body from receiving messages. What most of us don't realize is that we are the first line of defense against this onslaught of negative energy!

Accordingly, this negative energy can and will trigger a physical stress response in the body when one may not be warranted. While these stress response patterns serve as filters for protection from our environment, they can also distract our body from receiving the support it needs and messages that are crucial to our health and well-being. And when these stress response symptoms are experienced for the long term, the result is a series of biological reactions that activate in order to compensate for everything that has fallen out of sync. Essentially, our bodies become conditioned to function in a state of dis-function.

I failed to recognize my ability to defend against the onslaught of negative energy when I didn't see that the energetic mechanics that powered my body through a run were the same mechanics that created the crazy experience at the birth of my son and the same ones that were causing my migraines. While the overall quality of the energy (thoughts and food) that I put into my body was good, there were aspects that were compromised (medication, low sleep, lots of coffee, and limiting beliefs). Consequently, I could no longer manage the negative energies without serious side effects. I had reached my tipping point, where the negative energies were stronger and more profound than the positive ones.

Learning to see energy in life and understanding its laws and principles forms a foundation by which to structure thoughts and efforts. This process helped me build the bridge between the extreme, miraculous coincidences and the urgent need to bring about stress relief.

The Energy Positive Perspective

A NEW METHOD OF OBSERVATION

How do we observe what we cannot see?

Given that energy is important to our observations and transformation, we need to understand a bit more about it. And try to answer the difficult question: How do we observe what we cannot see?

Fortunately, science has postulated some enlightening answers:

1. Everything is Energy
2. Infinite Possibilities Abound
3. Energy Expands and Contracts
4. Everything Radiates a Unique Energetic Signature
5. Energy Lives Within Us: Thoughts and Emotions
6. Energy is Constantly Communicating
7. Energy Is Constantly Transforming.

The most beautiful and profound sensation we can experience is the sensation of the mystical. It is the power of all true science.

—Albert Einstein

The Energy Positive Perspective

1. Everything Is Energy

EVERYTHING IS ENERGY, in theory.

In the scientific world, observations are made and theories are postulated and tested to further understanding of universal energy. Albert Einstein's Theory of Relativity, E=MC(2), was the first idea to propose that "everything is energy." Since Einstein's work, quantum theorists have expanded the theory and begun to prove energy is the common link between everything we experience in life--from the thoughts we think to the words on this page, to the life we live and create.

But what is energy? Quantum theorists describe energy in its purest form as light. Light is further described by quantum theorists as both photons, which are particles of matter; and waves, which are packets of information. In other words, light is observed to act as both a solid (visible) and energy (invisible).

This energetic link is evidenced in the composition of the physical world: everything is made up of the exact same material--light, which—we now know is both particles and waves, visible and invisible, and energy and information. Furthermore this energy and information expresses an inherent ability to organize and orchestrate an infinite array of possibilities. At any given moment there is pure potential for these packets of information or light to vibrate in and out of consciousness.

These packets of information flash into existence, unite, and form the chemistry of bulk matter, which is everything from the stars to our physical bodies, thoughts and ideas. Inherent in this scientific formula, however, is the need for observation. Our simple ability to observe and desire creates intention; and, accordingly, elicits energy and information to form or manifest from the field of intelligence.

Think about it this way: Our thoughts are energy. Energy is light. Light is both a wave of information and a particle of matter. Therefore, our thoughts are information and matter. When we think a "thought," we are simply "experiencing" or "observing" information and matter vibrating into existence from a field of intelligence.

What this means:
As we observe this field of intelligence, it is the nature of our thoughts that determines what our observation will be.

Based on this scientific formula, we are the observers of the field of intelligence and we witness its desire to manifest miracles into existence.

E+ PERSPECTIVE: Do you see the energy in your life? Do you ever have a sense that you are part of something greater than just yourself? Recall a time when you were overwhelmed with emotion, surprise, and awe. In these moments, you may physically feel lighter, emotionally you feel inspired, and spiritually, everything is perfect. These are the moments when we are most aware of the energy and information around us.

The Energy Positive Perspective

2. Infinite Possibilities Abound

Within the energetic, quantum world our observations are based on the field of intelligence. The field of intelligence is comprised of multiple reasons, explanations, congruencies, synchronicities and repeated patterns, which all contribute to what we "see." Think of a spider web. A spider can traverse either one single thread, or utilize all of its legs to traverse the intricate, complex weaving of threads woven into its web.

Likewise, as observers of both an energetic, multi-dimensional world and a fixed linear world, we can traverse or observe the vast array of energies or options by recognizing multiple possibilities that co-exist and create our experiences. Or, we can choose to observe or traverse linear, singular thought patterns.

The singular route is deterministic and evidenced in Newtonian physics. We know our path because we traverse from point A to point B; the probability of traversing only from A to B is very high. Conversely, utilizing energetic observations provides a multi-dimensional, multi-possible point of reference--the result is never due to one specific thing. Therefore, the probability that we traverse directly from point A to point B diminishes. This slight adjustment in perspective, then, opens the door to a degree of uncertainty. Consider the following comparison of the Newtonian "if, then," sequencing and the quantum mechanics "infinite possibility" sequencing:

We all recognize that billiard balls follow trajectories or paths prescribed by simple mechanical laws. A ball moves in a straight line until it hits the wall or another ball. The very basis for the success of good pool players is their ability to judge precisely the path of each ball given the force with which they hit it. Although even a good player might misjudge the path taken by a ball, there is in principle one and only one path that each ball will take (assuming a perfectly smooth table, no air resistance, etc..). Newtonian physics views the entire universe, in a sense, as a game of billiards. Each atom in the universe is like a tiny billiard ball interacting with other billiard balls. Although the rules of this interaction are more complicated than those of billiard balls, we could in theory predict the entire history of the universe if we knew the initial positions and velocities of each particle at the very beginning. In other words, classical (Newtonian) mechanics is deterministic: if we know the initial state of some system (like a billiard table), we can predict with 100% accuracy its state at some future time. The only uncertainty comes from our inability to exactly know its initial state.

Comparatively, quantum mechanics offers the infinite possibility perspective:

...quantum mechanics says that physical laws, even the laws of mechanics, are inherently probabilistic (this is slightly imprecise language, since nondeterminism actually only emerges at measurement, not during free evolution, but to a layman, this picture is sufficiently valid). For instance, the Feynman path integral formulation of quantum mechanics states that unlike classical particles, which take only a single path, quantum particles take all paths simultaneously. "Normal paths" or ones that we associate with classical mechanics, have a high probability of occurring, whereas "bizarre paths" occur with very low probability. Nonetheless, all paths are taken with some finite (though possibly small) probability. To use our billiards illustration, a quantum mechanical billiard ball would not only travel in a straight line, it would also take a path in which it curves to the left, or to the right, or leaps off the table, or teleports into the living room, all at the same time. The probability of each non-classical path would be extremely small, but would not be zero. Therefore, it would be rigorously invalid to

say that any particular path, no matter how unlikely, was impossible.

The billiard analogy can be applied to all aspects of life including the choices we make, emotions we feel and thoughts we believe. Opening our minds to the possibility that we can access resources and ideas that exceed our current observations and understanding that we are an array of energies—not just a single one--enables us to release older, inefficient tools or observations. Recognizing the possibility that we don't have all of the answers, and that the "good" or "positive" aspects co-exist with the "bad" or "negative," empowers us to transform and move the negative energy. And, most important, empowers us to begin to recognize the possibility of miracles.

We now see the connection to miracles. Classical physics allowed materialists to claim that certain events were simply impossible "according to the laws of physics". Quantum mechanics rules out such an appeal. All we can say now is that some event is highly improbable "according to the laws of physics". But there is a world of difference between impossible and improbable. If something is truly impossible, I can ignore it. If something is merely improbable, I need to at least consider it.
(Shenvi)

Your personal point of power:
Wouldn't you rather access more information? The field of infinite potential is the intelligence that orchestrates the flow of life. One cell effortlessly replicates until millions of unique, highly specialized members of a cellular community create your body.

While the scope of the human mind is limited to thoughts and beliefs that we've acquired from past experience and observation, we do have access to this field of possibility, though we rarely "tune-in" to its wisdom. Observing energy is the key to accessing this infinite array of perspectives and intelligence, and activating a greater capacity for creativity and miracles.

E+ PERSPECTIVE: How much of your life do you spend thinking in linear terms? "If this happens, then I can do that"? Are you a fairly relaxed individual? Do you always just "know" things will work themselves out? Focusing on interconnections, instead of taking our "best guess" at singular solutions, is far more productive and opportunistic.

The Energy Positive Perspective

3. Energy Expands and Contracts

All energy is subject to expansion and contraction. As *accomplished* observers of a physical world, we understand how energy "moves." Within our body there are intricate, internal flow charts that decide which areas to energize and when. We can think of the flow of this energy as excitement, charge, attention, awareness, or simply a life force. Within the physical world we see such events as schools of fish swimming in perfect unison or of flocks of birds flying in perfect synchronization. We also see clouds forming and water rushing in a stream. And we feel hungry when our stomach is empty. The energy that synchronizes animals in nature or drives geographical events is the same energy that flows through your body and coordinates millions of processes.

Energy generally flows from a point of higher potential energy (for example, in batteries, the+ end) to a point of lower potential energy (the negative -end or ground). Whether the flow of energy is evidenced in a circuit breaker, traveling across a cell membrane, or in a heated exchange of thoughts and ideas, the energy is constantly exchanging. A great analogy to understand the flow of energy is to imagine a rockslide going down a cliff. The higher the cliff (the positive charge), the more energy the rocks will have when they hit the bottom (the negative charge). The height of the cliff is like the charge. The more rocks you have the more energy is being carried down the cliff. And the action of the rocks going through, say, some bushes on the way down is a method for losing energy in the flow process, as the impediment will use up energy.

In our body energy flows across membranes from higher to lower potential. All cells absorb or consume nutrients in the form of molecules, which represent charges:

> *Normally, the outside of a living cell has a positive electrical charge and the inside of a cell, a negative charge. But these charges may be momentarily reversed by the action of "ion pumps" on the cell membrane that drive sodium ions out of the cell and pump potassium ions into the cell (an ion is an atom or group of atoms that carries an electrical charge). This is the way that neurological impulses, for example, move along nerve cells.* (Eden, 2008)

Our thoughts are nothing more than charges moving across a cellular membrane. Foods we consume provide nothing more than nutrients to move across the cellular membrane.

We are all familiar with the physical sensation of consuming a lot of sugar, and then feeling bad. Emotions mimic this behavior as well: think of a day when you felt like you were "on top of the world," were you able to sustain that feeling indefinitely? Most likely not, as exhaustion or new events that trigger stress most likely interfered with sustaining your high point.

We witness energy moving in our bodies with modern technology. An EKG is an electrocardiogram that measures the electrical activity of the heart. An EEG is an electro-encephalogram that measures the brain's activity. And with an MRI, or Magnetic Resonance Imaging, we observe different parts of the body by viewing the electromagnetic field.

In our lives we witness people, events, and opportunities coming and going. Everything from our health, careers, thoughts and emotions are subject to a form of expansion and contraction.

In the environment the earth expands spring through summer and contracts fall through winter.

E+ PERSPECTIVE: Where in your life does energy flow from high to low? When you eat sugar, you experience a high and then a crash. When you are with a group of friends that you don't see often, you experience a "buzz" or high from the "good times," and then may experience "withdrawal." Where do you recognize energy expanding and contracting? Where do you see patterns in your life repeating? Expansion and contraction can be applied to the repetition of emotions, circumstances, thoughts and people we experience in our life. When was the last time you thought, "Why does this keep happening to me"?

When we step away from a scientific view, we find the movement of these energies has been analyzed and documented for thousands of years by spiritual systems that describe it as *chi, ki,* or *prana.* These systems analyze the energy flow through the body, and facilitate the movement of energy through the body by balancing the energy to release stress and symptoms.

The Energy Positive Perspective

4. Everything Radiates A Unique Energetic Signature
(Including You!)

What is an Energetic Signature?
Electricity and magnetism are closely related. Flowing electrons produce a magnetic field, and spinning magnets cause an electric current to flow. Electromagnetism is the interaction of these two important forces. Combined, these forces make up vortices of energy--an energetic signature.

Atoms are light; the light is vibrating and radiating energy. The vibration occurs at a specific frequency, which creates an energetic signature. This signature vibration contains and communicates information about the nature of the atom. For example, an atom of gold has 79 protons and an atom of silver has 47 protons. These are the respective energetic signatures.

The Human Energetic Signature:
In the body this energetic signature is represented by *various combinations of energies that activate your body's different physical systems (1) electrical energies, (2) electromagnetic energies, and (3) "subtle" energies.*

First: *Electricity involves the movement of electrons and protons. Like a miniature battery, every cell in the body stores and emits electricity. By the time an embryo is only four cells in size, an electrical gradient can be detected that starts switching on specific genes. Every breath you take, every muscle you move, every morsel of food you digest involves electrical activity. Likewise, your memories, feelings, and thoughts are encoded in patterns of tiny electrical impulses.* (Eden, 2008)

Second: Our thoughts and emotions are primarily responsible for dictating and guiding the electrical energies within our body. These thoughts and emotions do this by emitting a frequency that resonates throughout our body. As these energies vibrate and move, they create electromagnetic energy (which can be measured by science in an MRI).

Likewise, because of the body's electromagnetic field, we attract all like things with a similar energetic signature, including people, circumstances, and events.

Our third combination of energies is believed to exist outside the electromagnetic spectrum. There are devices that are at least sensitive to subtle energies. They can provide an assessment of the energy flowing through each meridian and the corresponding internal organs it feeds. Changes measured in light emissions emanating from the chakras and meridians correspond with the energetic shifts that follow meditation, acupuncture, qigong, and other energy healing treatments.

> *Subtle energies were described by Einstein as energies we know because of their effects but do not have the instruments to detect directly. Electromagnetism was in that category only 250 years ago. Its effects could be observed, but electromagnetism could not itself be measured....While subtle energies cannot move a needle on a gauge, many civilizations have known how to engage them to restore health and vitality.* (Eden, 2008)

How do we experience our Energetic Signature?

We experience electromagnetic and subtle energy in both our thoughts and our environment. Think of it this way: We understand that a computer's internet connection broadcasts a frequency or signal, which is represented in binary information that tells both the nature of the machine (contained in the IP address) and the type of information requested—just like the thoughts and intentions that make up our energetic signature. We choose the frequency we want by selecting a web address--or thinking certain thoughts. In return, we receive, or attract, frequencies through the pictures broadcast back onto our screen of life. If we change the web address, or our thoughts, we tune into a NEW frequency.

E+ PERSPECTIVE: Recognize the similarities between how energy behaves in your physical environment and within your own body. For example, your body, your thoughts, your emotions—everything you experience--is energy; and, therefore, subject to the laws of physics.

This means that you:

- Are magnetic and able to attract things into your life.
- Have a frequency you project into the environment, and influence those around you, depending on whether you exhibit a higher or lower charge. You may feel expansive around some people and withdrawn around others.
- Receive frequencies so your energy is constantly expanding and contracting according to the contact with which it comes into contact.
- Will lose energy when exposed to prolonged, unfavorable frequencies. Think of a person who always "drains" your

energy or the physiological impact of living under power lines.

- Receive grounding energies from the earth and inspirational energies from your environment.
- Can interfere with an energetic system in your body. Acupuncture and chiropractic procedures are popular examples of restoring lost energy.
- Can be influenced by "group" thoughts; the best example being the media. When an idea gets projected, many people begin to receive the signal; and the greater number who hear the signal, the stronger it becomes and the greater its impact.

The Energy Positive Perspective

5. How Energy Lives Within Us
Emotions & Thoughts

EMOTIONS: Energy in motion = e-motion.

Emotions are energy and information for our body. Our body utilizes emotions as a means to send "group messages" throughout our entire body. Our mind coordinates with the limbic system to achieve this feat by converting "molecules" that transfer across a cell membrane into "feelings" or physical sensations. Emotions or "group messages" are then sent and received as a group at every level of the body, including cellular and within the brain.

To be effective, emotions have a very powerful "charge" around them. Consider telling a friend about a terrifying experience that happened to you. Not only will you experience your fear or get the "chills" as you recount the events, but most likely your friend will also. We experience other people's emotions all the time. Think of walking into a hostile room or walking through the gates at your favorite amusement park. Or, we often describe a bar or a restaurant as having a "great feel to it." In all of these circumstances we are observing the emotional charge that was experienced there.

Emotions always occur because of interaction with the environment. If you are walking down a dark alley in the middle of the night, you may experience fear. Your heightened sense of fear is cuing every cell in your body to be ready to run. In the reverse, imagine you are at the beach on a sunny, pleasant day off from work; there is a great breeze, and you are listening to the waves roll onto the shore. You are relaxed, happy and content.

In both cases the emotions are created by your body in response to a "trigger" in your environment. You are experiencing the energy of the emotion; the emotions flowing through your body are being processed or consumed on a cellular level, and creating an emotional "charge" around the thoughts you have.

Emotions are a form of communication from your body. When you feel good, you "know" you are interacting with your environment in a positive way. You are most likely experiencing expansion. When you are feeling bad, you are most likely in a contraction mode. Your emotions are the signals that indicate how the "overall" energy in your body is moving.

Emotions also indicate where energy has stopped moving in our bodies:

Emotions can be defined as the energy that moves us. Considering that energy is always in motion, when we internalize, deny or disconnect from an emotion, that energy takes a wrong turn that often keeps us stuck in a maze. Every time internalized, denied or disconnected emotions are triggered, the body becomes compromised and has to compensate, leaving it at risk for injury or opportunistic pathogens. Recurrent symptoms and chronic stress are the warning signs that emotions are trapped within the subconscious mind. (Weissman, 1997)

E+ PERSPECTIVE: Recognize the Expression and Flow of Emotions

Where do emotions live in your body? If you are anxious, do you get sick to your stomach? When emotions flow, energy is flowing. When emotions are blocked or suppressed because they are too traumatic to experience them—or we think we don't have time to "deal" with them--we essentially send the message to our body to store the "charge" of the emotion until a later date. But, if we don't deal with such emotions, we can expect to experience resulting symptoms.

THOUGHTS ARE ENERGY FLOWING THROUGH YOU

Every thought you experience is a form of energy moving and expressing itself. Thoughts were born out of the need to communicate and coordinate "advanced" signals (in the form of molecules)—or messages to the entire body. A "thought" is simply the result of multiple messages or information concerning the environment being filtered, prioritized, stored and processed at all levels within the body. From the cell, all the way up to our brain, thoughts are energy exchanging information.

The layered nature of the nervous system creates individual thought or processing centers throughout the body. Utilizing this layered network, the body is able to respond to the environment quickly and efficiently. These intricate layers of processing also allow for multiple messages—or "primitive thoughts"--from your cellular communities (e.g., heart and lung cells) to send messages via the nervous system regarding conditions in their respective environments. These signals, depending on priority, are processed and then responded to with a message sent back via the nervous system.

Thoughts are simply energy and information flowing that happen to be structured in the context of language. Thoughts originate in the pre-frontal cortex of the brain. As humans, we think of thoughts as a unique and personal experience. But in reality, the thoughts we experience in our own consciousness occur everywhere in our environment. Our conscious mind simply serves as an evolved sense organ, which is tasked with making outside observations of all energy being processed within the body and the environment, and then coordinating a response to those stimuli.

E+ PERSPECTIVE: Do you think of thoughts as energy? Do you recognize how our cells are influenced by our thoughts? Do you recognize the power of "nourishing" your cells with "positive" or higher-charged thoughts?

Kari Caldwell

The Energy Positive Perspective

6. Energy Constantly Communicates
(Your Job is to Listen)

Imagine your body is an advanced computer, a "bio-computer." Within your bio-computer system, symptoms, events, and people are the means by which the energy communicates. As the "user," your job is to interpret and respond according to the information you receive. While your physical body speaks through the language of symptoms and emotions, your energy speaks through events and people that are attracted into your life.

When your beliefs are congruent with the natural flow of energy in your environment, events and people and relationships that are highly rewarding appear. The feedback from your environment and experience of it may be "You are on the right track," or "That was amazing, let's do it again." Conversely, when you hit bumps in the road, experience hardship or disagreement in your life, your body is essentially saying, "You have a limiting belief," "Your potential is greater than this," or, "You have a valuable life lesson or 'golden nugget' waiting for you."

E+ PERSPECTIVE: Do you recognize the messages your energy is sending and receiving? Do you recall a person or resource showing up at just the right moment? Or conversely, something being taken out of your life in sequence with other events occurring?

The Energy Positive Perspective

7. Energy Constantly Transforms

Energy never ceases to be in motion. Even when it is blocked, it transforms into something else. Remember the rockslide going down the cliff. The more rocks you have, the more energy you have to carry down the cliff, and the more bushes you have to crush.

But what is actually happening when energy transforms?

We know energy in its purest form is light. And light acts as both matter and a wave. And the wave is packets of information. We can then think of the packets as moving particles that force the matter to vibrate at different levels or frequencies. When the wave forces the particle to vibrate at a different frequency, it does so incrementally, which means there is no in between. The photon must either go up or down. In other words, the movement of the wave photons forces a particle to experience a different level, and transform and change its nature.

Recall the nature of energy flowing in cells where ion pumps move positive and negative charges across the cell membrane. In this case, the cell is transformed by the "molecule" that transfers across the membrane.

When we relate the nature of transformation to our thoughts and emotions, we recognize that the thought, which is a form of matter, can directly influence the "frequency" of the environment in which it exists. Therefore, the very nature of observing and the quality of the "thought" or "observation" while seemingly insignificant, is in fact highly impactful on the nature of our experience—or reality.

E+ PERSPECTIVE: Where do you recognize your ideas and thoughts being influenced by people and your environment. Is this a positive or negative influence? Do you find yourself responding physically to these energies? Maybe you feel excitement or maybe you feel so disgusted you are physically ill?

Kari Caldwell

PART 1

SUMMARY

THE ENERGY YOU ALREADY RECOGNIZE:

Consider recognizing the Energy Positive Perspective: our thoughts are evidence of our body processing and storing information; our emotions are evidence of our body interacting and responding to experiences in life; and our observations are interpretations of energy moving around us.

The more you recognize the Energy Positive perspective in your life, the more "energetic" your life will become, and the more you will experience:

- New patterns and movement of energy
- How to co-create opportunities with the "intelligent energy"
- How to observe negative states more keenly, and to better prepare yourself to handle them
- How to mitigate the "negativity" in your life so it has less impact on your decisions.

Most importantly you will transform your negative thought patterns, from restriction, bad energy, sadness, and loss of hope to opposite feelings of worthiness, abundance, joy and hopefulness.

PART TWO

Strategies for creating an Energy Postive+ Life

Kari Caldwell

You may control a mad elephant;
You may shut the mouth of the bear and the tiger;
Ride the lion and play with the cobra;
By alchemy you may learn your livelihood;
You may wander through the universe incognito;
Make vassals of the gods; be ever youthful;
You may walk in water and live in fire;
But control of the mind is better and more difficult.

> –Paramahansa Yogananda,
> Autobiorgraphy of a Yogi

Kari Caldwell

PART II

Strategies: Creating an Energy Positive+ Life

Have you ever watched an event unfold and thought, "This isn't happening. How did I get to this place? My life and this scenario cannot be real." Have you examined the series of events throughout your life that built the current circumstance?

Maybe it was a bad decision when you were a kid. Maybe you've had to default on a debt due to an unforeseen circumstance, or maybe you lost the love of your life. Perhaps you made all the right decisions, but life still just turned upside down. Maybe you feel like you've changed and nothing makes sense in the way it did before. Whatever your negative circumstance, you can't seem to find a way out--a satisfactory path to a better place.

Identifying the link that brought on your current woes seems overwhelming and complex. And, it happened fast. Almost in the blink of an eye, your world has transformed around you. Your marriage, your kids, your family, your home, and your livelihood have all been affected. And you know the changes are not necessarily for the better.

Within one month of my first son being born, my husband and I lost our home to Hurricane Wilma. Despite our best laid plans, our lives over the course of a 72-hour period were changed drastically. I will never forget sitting with my newborn in my arms, staring into his eyes, knowing I intended to give him better, yet not having a single word to say. I was lost. I wondered how the stress and shock I was experiencing was going to affect him. I comforted myself with the knowledge that we were safe, warm, and with plenty of food and most important, love. But it did not change the fact that I knew deep inside that my son was experiencing the grief also.

It wouldn't be until many years later that I began to understand how that grief we shared in those first months of his life would influence him. In hindsight, that hurricane was my first event to mark the beginning of my perfect storm that was brewing. It would be a long road wrought with equally challenging circumstances that strained my relationships with myself, my husband and my family.

But in the midst of my chaos, and at the risk of sounding cliché, I received a unique and special gift—it seemed a miracle. My ray of light came in the form of an idea:

Everything is energy and energy is everything; therefore, we live in an energetic world where anything is possible for all forms of life when intention, perseverance, and faith are applied. Energy empowered me to change my choices.

It is a simple concept that buoyed my faith in my ability to transform my situation. Learning to embody its principles kept me afloat in my despairing moments; and, ultimately, taught me how to swim to calmer waters.

I encourage you to consider your personal, first-hand experience with energy. We all know the terms--karma, prana, chi, and God. And we all know what a "good vibration" feels like. Energy is around you everywhere. It is in the symbols that charge the words on this page into thoughts and also a voice inside your head. It is in the chair in which you are sitting, and it is in the past and in the future. How can you embrace this energy to achieve what you want out of life?

Kari Caldwell

STRATEGIES: CREATING AN ENERGY POSITIVE+ LIFESTYLE

DEFINITION:

AN ENERGY POSITIVE+ LIFE:

A state of being where expansive and regenerative energies within your awareness are greater than their respective counterparts.

We all have assets. And we all use our proverbial toolbox to build our assets. Most of us think of assets as fixed things or objects—and they are—in the physical world. But when we transition into the quantum, energetic world, we are carried from the surface level to the multi-dimensional energetic asset. Energetic assets are timeless and permanent in nature. And when our positive energetic assets are greater than their negative counterparts, we recognize an Energy Positive Life.

Energetic assets consist of your dreams and intentions; they are comprised of an intricate web of the energies we experience in life, such as, love, abundance, happiness, fear, excitement, sadness, health, creativity, inspiration and joy. When we focus on our energetic assets, we connect with infinite intelligence, possibility and opportunity.

Unlike their physical counterparts, energetic assets come in many forms, such as emotions, experiences, or coincidences. Regardless of appearance, energetic assets represent the cumulative outcome of our intentions.

THE NAUTRE OF OUR POWER

In the Introduction we discussed our proverbial toolbox that we try to build and fill with "tools," which are strengths, coping mechanisms or strategies, over our lifetime. These tools help us meet our daily and long-term challenges. They represent the source of our power—our inherent ability to be strong, confident and in control of our energetic assets.

The main reason we all typically search to find the "right" strategies for our personal use is that we need strong and reliable abilities to adjust to the never-ending expansion and contraction that occurs in our physical world. Our world is always moving and transforming; the physical aspects of our life, such as people, relationships, and possessions, inevitably expand and contract; they come and go.

While we don't control this expansion and contraction—or the existence of the energies themselves, we do have the power to control our personal experience of it.

THE TIPPING POINT

Our goal then becomes to utilize these energetic strategies to tip our overall energy into an Energy Positive state of being, where the positive expansive and regenerative energies are greater than their respective counterparts.

Utilizing our power to choose expansion breathes light and energy into the seeds of our intentions and desires. But more important, it allows for the energies around us to freely flow. Power over this freedom of movement, however, also includes the negative, contractive energies. Our ability to allow both the negative and positive energies to pour forth facilitates more and greater experiences with the positive aspects of any single energy.

It is only when our power is compromised that our experience of our intentions is diminished. The following strategies are designed to help you reclaim your power by focusing on the expansive aspects of your positive energies. This focusing facilitates the streaming of your energy, and re-establishes balance by diffusing and redirecting your experience of "negativity" or contraction.

LITTLE BOOK OF ENERGY

STRATEGIES: CREATING AN ENERGY POSITIVE+ LIFE

BUILDING ENERGY INTO ASSETS,

RECLAIMING YOUR POWER

STRATEGY 1: CHANGE YOUR CHOICE, RECLAIM YOUR POWER

STRATEGY 2: DREAM BIG

STRATEGY 3: OWN YOUR STORY

STRATEGY 4: FUEL YOUR ENERGY BODY

STRATEGY 5: PRACTICE, PRACTICE, PRACTICE

STRATEGY 6: EXPECT MIRACLES

The Energy Positive strategies are plans of action to help you reclaim your power, build your assets, and reinforce an Energy Positive+ Life by

- Keeping negative energy flowing

- Attracting and engaging positive energy

- Strengthening the presence and your experience of positive energy

- Incorporating the energy practices into your daily life.

Primarily, though, you will learn to convert all of your energies--whether expanding or contracting-- into your most valuable assets of your proverbial toolbox. And learn to utilize these assets to experience success, abundance, love, joy and miracles.

Your task is not to seek for love, but merely seek and find all the barriers within yourself that you have built against it.

—Rumi

Kari Caldwell

Strategy 1:

Change Your Choice, Reclaim Your Power

Purpose: Reclaim Your Power

What to Do with the Negative: Look For Evidence

How to: Change Your Choice: Incremental Steps to Own Your Power

Strategy 1:

Change Your Choice, Reclaim Your Power

Have you ever been faced with a decision that has an obvious path, but somehow choosing that path brings forth some kind of gut instinct that it might be the wrong one? You're not sure, but acknowledge to yourself that it might contain inherent flaws. This dilemma is not unusual. In such a situation, we often cannot identify the source of our unrest, however, it's definitely there. Despite this sense, though, if we have valid and justified reasons and good purpose and intention to choose this path, we feel compelled to do so.

Inherently, making our choice is our power. And generally, any nagging sensation about the choice is our power tugging at our sleeve, saying, "WARNING! You are about to relinquish some control over this situation!"

Sometimes, we may want to relinquish this control intentionally to fulfill a greater purpose, but sometimes we are not aware of choosing to relinquish it. But, whatever our reason, once our power is gone, it can be a slippery and complicated journey to reclaim it.

A very close friend once found himself in a very "sticky" predicament. He had left a well-paid, top corporate job with a glamorous title to pursue an entrepreneurial dream with a highly trusted associate. Six months into the endeavor, however, values and morality became an issue. My friend was left with no choice but to leave. Having just moved his family, and not wanting to re-enter corporate life so soon, he felt out of options. Weeks of deliberation and contemplation of self-worth ensued; inevitably, he realized he needed to--in his words--"change his choice." Instead of following the traditional road of re-entry into the corporate world, he chose a less traveled path: He and his wife sold some assets, and embarked on a road trip around the country for several months. They spent this time visiting friends and reaching out to any and all acquaintances and connections within their network. During their journey, ideas were formed and an alternative, positive solution presented itself, which fulfilled both of their needs.

Changing your choice is one of the most powerful tools we possess. It is the tool that empowers us to reclaim any and all power we have lost. While we may not think we have the opportunity to effect drastic changes in our choices like my friend did, we always have a choice. We just have to push beyond all those multiple stories we tell ourselves that keep us locked into certain pathways that we know aren't working. I encourage you to open your eyes to the choices you make, and to recognize where and how you relinquish your power. Even if you are not able or willing to make significant changes, simple awareness of the power you have ultimately empowers you to find alternative options to move forward and reclaim what is rightfully yours.

CROSSROADS

In the course of our day-to-day life, we make many decisions; some are major, such as where to attend college or which job to pursue; others are minor, such as what to have for breakfast. Either way, these moments represent our "crossroads," and can have great consequences. But even though we don't always see the significance of every choice and decision we've ever made or every action we've ever taken, it is still important because we are exercising our most special gift: free will.

Our ability to freely choose means we control our experience of any situation or energy; we control our power, and can both promote positive expansion and control contraction. Every choice is essentially a crossroads with paths that either lead us toward our intentions or away from them.

Get the energy flowing with choice. Every choice we make is a mechanism or opportunity to move or facilitate the flow of an energy. Often, we fail to recognize this relationship between the "smaller" choice and the greater "theme," because we make choices from a physical, limited perspective, focusing only on the "if, then" sequencing. When you examine a routine such as brushing your teeth from this physical perspective, there is no energy to correlate or reinforce this relationship. The energetic perspective, on the other hand, creates greater opportunity—and requires less effort to recognize and facilitate the flow of energy in our lives. While it may be hard to ascertain the deeper significance of a simple act like choosing to brush your teeth, consider what you are doing when you "simply" brush your teeth: you exercise self-care which is a form of love. And the "experience of love" is an intention. This little act of love is easy to overlook. However, if your intention is to build the experience of love in your life, your choice to give yourself "love" and intentionally recognize that you are "experiencing love," reinforces the energy of having love. In turn, if we pay *significant* attention to the self-love choice of brushing our teeth, we will ultimately attract more and greater "experiences of love."

The Energy Positive Perspective is based upon the premise that there are infinite possibilities. Therefore, if you are seemingly "stuck" in a situation, there is conceivably an alternative that exists at some level within your being; you just can't see it. The key is not to try to "know" the path or the exact action steps to take. Rather, the key is to look for and find evidence or proof of your desired alternative option at its point of inception, the intention. After all, if you choose to believe it exists, then it does. In every moment, you can choose to believe the alternative exists, whether you "see" evidence of it or not. The more you choose the energy and make choices to support it in your physical experience, the stronger the energy will become, and a greater likelihood of discovering your path will exist. In most cases, we already have physical experience of our intentions. We just choose not to support them.

FINDING YOUR ALTERNATIVE.

But what do we do when we don't recognize our opportunities to choose? Our lives are a compilation of energies that are constantly ebbing and flowing in and out of existence—or expanding and contracting. This constant movement creates a rhythm and flow of both negative and positive energies. With this constant motion, and constant opportunity for choice, the best energy to focus on is not always obvious. Additionally, we become so absorbed in a certain belief or energy that we are incapable of seeing our alternative options.

Crossroads that we avoid

Consider a difficult situation or challenge that you struggle to overcome. Perhaps it is related to finances, a relationship or career. But even if the situation is insignificant, the issue becomes one of not being able to identify a solution. In this case, if you can't find your path, and you can't see the alternative, how do you find the "crossroads," when the decision point doesn't seem to exist? You may encounter the advice, "Just believe you already have what you are seeking." But how do you find the positive alternative, peace and calm in the midst of feeling negative energy? Or how do you believe and act like you have an abundance of money, when you struggle to put food on the table? How do you shift your mindset and release limiting beliefs when your present experience is so incredibly incongruent with your desired solution?

Moving negative energies is a monumental feat. And to move them, they must be acknowledged to some degree. Many people spend lifetimes avoiding negative energies. And understandably so; we almost have to let ourselves be bystanders to our own lives to bear the pain that can come with experiencing such negative emotions as grief, loss, and shame. Inevitably though, negative energies will ebb and flow; and despite our best efforts to avoid them, we will always be forced to stand face-to-face with them until we muster the courage to transform them.

If we don't change our darker energies and alter their path, we will continue to find ourselves out of balance and perhaps in pain, looking for the crossroads. When these negative energies form a cycle of repeating, we experience the most pain. Not only do we open old wounds, but we experience profound shame for seemingly recreating the same mistake. Shame is something we learn when we try to understand or make our "best guess" and fail—we believe we should have done or known better. It is one of the hardest energies to move because by its nature it implies that we are not worthy of more or "better."

Courage. Courage is what we find when we feel out of options and not yet at our crossroads. Our courage comes from the inner knowing that we can't go any further on the path we are walking.

We must choose to take a risk. We must choose to be vulnerable. We must choose to stop judging ourselves. We must choose to release our shame and negativity. Most important, we must choose to release the need to control and the subsequent responsibility that accompanies it.

A world of abundance. Courage also comes from the belief that we live in a world of abundance and love, and not in a world that harbors shame or is centered around absence. Humanity has not evolved to the current state of consciousness because of absence. Our crossroads emerges from the belief that we can either choose a life of abundance and love or not. When we choose love, the other negative beliefs of shame and unworthiness become untruths. We are able to recognize them as self-judgments that we've formed, based upon our limited awareness or understanding. When we recognize love and abundance, we recognize that we are not qualified to make these judgments, and that some of our "best-guesses" could possibly be inaccurate. By the natural laws of physics, the energy you are experiencing must have an opposite.

We must. When we reach this crossroads, it is almost as if we hear a voice in our head saying, "I can't. I can't. I can't." It is in the midst of these "I can'ts" that an inner knowing rises from deep inside saying, "I must." This force is driven by our belief in abundance. It calls from beyond the raw, dark pain and encourages us to move forward. While we cannot see the force, we are able to sense it looming on the other side of our pain. Our hearts, although battered and broken, are drawn to it.

Surrender. When you accept that you are willing to listen to the "I must," inevitably your alternative path will be illuminated. We will receive the tools and resources we need; we will discover the abundance of love, forgiveness and compassion that is rightfully ours.

In this moment of experiencing surrender, we find the need for our crossroads; we find our moment of choice. We can choose to surrender, and give our full attention to the energies, allowing the grief, shame, guilt, and loss to flow freely through our soul. In these moments we can acknowledge every little limiting belief. We learn the depth of our pain, the depth of our loss, and the depth of our grief. In this most vulnerable time we finally recognize our choice: we can either continue to harbor these emotions inside, or we can surrender to the truth and ask for love to be ushered into our lives to heal our pain.

While our minds may not "know" this alternative, as soon as we make this choice, we discover love. Ever so slightly, the burden is lifted, and we discover a greater purpose—we recognize that we truly do not control the ebb and flow of energy. We are simply observers of it. Our negative emotions come from the belief that we are responsible or have control—but we don't have any such control. We simply facilitate these energies to expand. This awareness enables us to look at our negativity from the outside. We no longer need to ignore or deny it, because we realize it is not our job to carry it. And most important, when we choose to believe in the power of abundance and love in these moments, we recognize that nothing is ever taken away without receiving a greater reward.

Illumination. Our choice illuminates our deepest desires and intentions. And in these instances when the seeds of our intentions are sewn, we find our commitment, our desire and our purpose. As our "best-guesses" fade into the light, our intentions rise from a deep slumber. Our job is to choose to build the energies of these positive intentions.

We may question which aspects of our lives support our intentions and which do not. For example, do you continue a relationship or activity that you like but that triggers old energy patterns? Do you continue to spend your savings or incur further debt to promote the flow of money energies or to gain valuable insight through education? The answers are unique to each of us. And the only way we truly "know" the right path is to be very clear about how each of the alternatives supports or detracts from our intentions.

CHANGE YOUR CHOICE: Incremental steps to reclaim your power!

Choose something different. When was the last time you did something different just for the "heck of it"? As humans, we are incredibly habitual and predictable creatures. Although we have one of the most phenomenal tools, free choice, we rarely use it. If you aren't certain about where to begin or how to create change, start changing your habits. Try driving home from work a different way, getting up five minutes earlier, calling an old friend, or eating a food that you would normally never choose.

Changing your choices is the easiest way to create an entirely new influx of energy. It creates a new force that makes you unpredictable, and, accordingly, opens tiny windows of opportunity for new movement to be ushered into your life.

Choose different emotions. This is very simple advice that is more difficult to implement than it seems. Try controlling your road rage; frustration of waiting in a line for a slow cashier; or kids not listening to you. If you can identify an alternative thought pattern and choose to experience patience instead, you instantly engage in supporting an energy that is in greater alignment with your intentions.

Choose to be bad. Sometimes, we just have to intentionally do something we shouldn't. There is a freedom that comes with harmless acts of naughtiness! We spend a lot of time complying with social norms, so at times instead of following your neat and orderly day, try doing something "out of character." Maybe you leave work early for no reason. Maybe you take an extra-long lunch and get a pedicure—without feeling guilty. Maybe you sleep in all day and serve your kids breakfast for dinner. Whatever your "bad' behavior is, make the most of it. Have guilt free fun and feel rewarded and energized by the influx of new energies you attract during your day.

Choose what is real right now. Our choice only exists in the present moment. But how often do we make decisions for the future or for the past? Of course we evaluate past probabilities in order to calculate future realities. But in the present moment, you can only choose and influence what is immediately at hand. A choice made in the present doesn't change the past and the only way to influence the future is with your choice right now.

When we choose in the moment, we get to choose immediately what makes us the happiest, most content, or full of love. We receive instant gratification and recognize fulfillment. Every moment that we do not choose these energies, we are cheating ourselves.

Choose gratitude and love. When all else fails, the emotions of gratitude and love will transform any situation, no matter how unbearable. These energies are expansive and will halt the contraction of sadness and grief instantly.

CHANGE YOUR CHOICE: CHOOSE OUTSIDE THE BOX!

A friend of mine had been working on his marriage for years. Despite intensive counseling and repeated discussions, he and his wife could not manage to communicate effectively on some big issues. Although committed, it became increasingly clear to him that their lives were out of balance and growing apart.

In one of their heated discussions, his wife gave him three options for how they could return harmony and balance to their relationship.

It was abundantly clear to him, however, that the more committed he was to fulfilling his intentions, the more improbable it would be to experience happiness in his marriage. He decided to choose outside the box. As he puts it, "She laid out options A,B, and C, and I chose Option D."

SUMMARY:

ATTRIBUTES OF CHOICE:

You control your choices; therefore, you control your response to events in your life, and can direct the energy for your future experiences.

Utilizing choice empowers us to influence the natural "process" of energies expanding and contracting around us.

The more you change your choices, the more you will receive opportunities for making new choices.

Choices give us the power to both create new energy and remove old energy.

There is no "wrong" or "right" choice.

Choices should be guided by intentions, not by limiting beliefs or misperceptions of the past or future.

Kari Caldwell

When your mind is narrow small things agitate you easily. Make your mind an ocean.

–Lama Thubten Yeshe

Kari Caldwell

Strategy 2:

Dream Big

Purpose: Expand your energy

What to Do with the Negative: Dreams Don't Die, Dreams Transform

How to: Dream Big

STRATEGY 2: DREAM BIG

Infinite possibilities. Were you blessed as a young person to have a parent who told you that you could accomplish anything? I was, yet even being told this, I still unintentionally managed to limit myself. My limitations came mostly from an ignorance of what was available. Acquired limitations stemmed from beliefs I learned, such as not fitting in socially, to thinking I shouldn't join a certain team because I was a girl. As kids, we dream and envision our lives unfolding in a grand manner. But as adults, these dreams tend to shift toward such goals as getting a good job, education, finding a lifelong partner. We seem to lose touch with the freedom that comes from thinking of ourselves as infinite and able to accomplish anything. Ask yourself how often you think of yourself as limitless.

Even after having learned the energetic concept of infinite possibilities, I still struggle to grasp its full meaning. My mind easily devises stories, scenarios, and explanations for why the seemingly impossible should be possible. Yet, I remain committed to understanding the implications of believing that absolutely anything is possible in my life.

Initially, I conceived the idea that I could win the lottery. Of course, why not? Accordingly, I dedicated a lot of time writing out the dreams that I would fulfill if I were to win the lottery. It was a long list. The interesting thing was, in the process, I began to recognize where in my life I already experienced what I was seeking.

I also discovered that I had quite a few limiting beliefs concerning money. So, it made sense to believe that what prevented me from recognizing my dreams was money. The irony is that I had enough money to do what I wanted at the moment, like stop working after having three children. In hindsight, I would not define my relationship with money as healthy. I now see how much power I handed over to limiting beliefs around wealth. Somewhere along the way I learned to fear not having enough of it; this could have stemmed from family lore about the Depression. Accordingly, this energy of scarcity would occasionally "pop" up in my life to justify and support my belief that money energy was scarce.

The more I strategized and dreamed, the more my dreams transitioned from being about experiencing a specific event to just experiencing the energy of it. I was able to release the exact outcome for the energy of the dream. I also began to have greater appreciation for the aspects of my dreams that I was already experiencing. For example, laughter and love were top on my list. I began to really pay attention to what was happening when my kids, husband and I would enjoy a hilarious moment. Essentially, all of the little details helped me build my path toward my seemingly "impossible" dreams.

Dreaming big sounds like a terrific idea, but it can be a really scary endeavor. To fully achieve it, you have to be willing to be vulnerable. As you work your way through your dreams, your mind does an excellent job of analyzing all of the reasons why you are not qualified or worthy of your heart's greatest desire. This vulnerability essentially exposes you to your self-worth and doubt. The concept of infinite possibilities grounded me in these times of doubt. Achieving your dreams and recognizing your intentions is not about you; you recognize them because you simply accept the greatness of infinite possibilities that lives within you. After all, our world is abundant and we are all intended to receive an abundance of possibilities and energies. Therefore, the trick is to figure out how to transform whatever beliefs and energies stand between you and the abundance you want to recognize.

INTENTIONS

When was the last time you considered your intentions? In our fast-paced world, we do not devote a lot of time and focus on intention. But, if you consider your reason for any and all thoughts and actions, intention is the driving force. Intentions are the source or cause of all desire and action. We may confuse an intention with a goal. When we set a goal or conceive a dream, we are seeking to fulfill an intention—or to experience a certain energy. For example, we may dream of meeting the perfect mate and falling in love; our goal is to meet the perfect mate in order to fulfill the intention to experience love.

Working with intentions is like deciding to take a trip. We start the process thinking we want to "go somewhere," but actually we are seeking to have the experience of being on a journey. We select our destination based on the type of experience we are seeking. If our "intention" is relaxation we may choose a beach destination. But if our "intention" is adventure, we may choose a hiking expedition or travel to a foreign country. During the planning stage, our focus remains on where we want to go and what we will see. We are driven to plan certain activities based upon our belief that those activities will help us fulfill our "intentions." Similarly, our dreams serve as a rough outline and "destination" for life.

Once our trip begins, the actual "journey" starts to unfold. We fulfill our intentions in the process of our experiencing our vacation—or journey—not just when we physically arrive at our end point. Inherent in this journey, though, are other experiences and energies. Maybe you thought it would be beneficial to travel with a friend, but once your journey begins, you recognize that your friend is not a great travel companion. Or upon arriving at your destination, you are less than satisfied with the accommodations. Experiencing our intentions in life is also wrought with other "unintended" energies.

Our intentions serve as the energetic "seeds" of our dreams that drive us to connect with our "greatest desires." When you conceive a dream, you attempt a "best-guess" as to how to fulfill your intentions or "greatest desires." You then begin to set goals or an agenda according to your "best guess" or dream.

These "best-guesses" are our attempt to fulfill an intention. Our dreams serve as a navigational tool that guides our decisions and actions. We utilize them to expand our ability to recognize the energy of an intention--without the trip, we may never experience the adventure or relaxation. Without our dreams we would never believe it possible or strive to incorporate new positive energies into our lives.

The pursuit of our dreams gives us the context or "platform" to fulfill an intention. As we pursue our dreams, we begin to recognize the energies we wish to experience. Recognizing the energies may seem insignificant and small at first, but gradually, as we continue the pursuit, the experience of the energies intensifies. The more we focus on the experience of an intention, instead of the achievement of a dream, the more successful we feel—and the more we attract the intended energy.

Leave the door open. Infinite Possibilities. To dream BIG not only means to identify and outline specifics of your greatest desires, but also to open your mind to the possibility that your experience of the dream be recognized beyond the scope of your imagination. In other words, by not limiting ourselves to the dreams in our minds, we expand our potential experience of our dreams to allow for the intelligent domain to supply the details and options.

Focus on the intention, not the outcome. In order for the intelligent domain to supply the "details," we need to release the "expected" outcome. Consider your trip, as you encounter the journey with a perspective of "no matter what happens it will all work out." With this attitude details do generally work out—and often for the better. If you maintain a focus that avoids adhering to exact planning, you can be confident that all of your needs, desires, and physical details will be recognized in the process of fulfilling your intentions.

Whether you are seeking to fulfill an intention on a trip or one in the bigger scheme of life, energy is always fulfilling something. Your ability to expect greater rewards than you can imagine, combined with your ability to release the outcome and "know" you will always experience the best, ensures that the energies being fulfilled do so with minimal interruption.

DREAMS DON'T DIE, DREAMS TRANSFORM

The perceived need to let go of a dream is due to its physical attributes. We often perceive loss because the human mind is far too limited to comprehend and calculate all the options and foresee all of the angles available to maintain the "life" of a dream. While a dream is limited to the laws of the physical domain, the energy of the dream--the seed of intention—never dies. Focusing on the intention when a dream seemingly "dies" or contracts, helps us determine how to best keep the energy flowing or expressing itself. While there may be adjustments in the physical domain, including feeling grief or other negative emotions, ultimately, the human soul's "greatest desires" will seek to express themselves again. And we will find other avenues to carry an energy forward, whether it is in memory, or creating purpose for the greater good.

DREAM BIG

Step One: Identify your intentions.

Do you seek to feel happiness, love, fulfillment, better health, laughter, creativity? Your intentions are the energies you want to experience in your life. Do not limit the scope of energies you seek. Write about them and imagine yourself feeling them.

Step Two: Identify your dreams and do not limit them! There are no bounds. You just need to ask!

Forget all of your present circumstances. If you could make something happen, what would you want to occur? Who would be in your life? Where would you be living? What would you be doing? Be very specific. Be very creative. Be very imaginative.

Step Three: As you formulate your dreams and intentions, consider an equal exchange of energy.

Step Four: Identify within your dreams what energies or intentions are being fulfilled.

Step Five: Recognize where your dreams are limited. Then, release the actual outcome or expectations you have around your dreams. And hold the space or believe that you will receive something even better than you imagined.

Step Six: Visualize and pace yourself. We don't usually experience "zero to sixty" overnight. Building anything starts small. To achieve your dreams, you have to start with the basic building blocks--the intentions you seek to have fulfilled. For example, you may not "feel happy" right now. But your belief that you will "feel happy," combined with your awareness of your dreams, will attract happiness into your life. We don't experience energy in the future; we experience it in the present. Your belief that you will feel the energy is the actual first experience of it. Your progression from commitment to believing, to choosing, and then to creating each experience in day-to-day living, is the critical foundation for building and strengthening the energy.

Step Seven: Once you embody the "belief" that you will achieve your dreams, make choices that support the belief. For example, if you are stressed about paying a big bill because you do not have sufficient funds, first evaluate all of your options; then choose the option that will not cause you to experience the same stress again. Essentially, when we do this, we are establishing a boundary around the experience of a particular energy. We are reclaiming our power over that energy, and ultimately, transforming the essence of the situation. I realize that in this circumstance the choice that eliminates the stressor may not be the favorable choice, however, reclaiming your power over an energy ensures that other negative energies fall into alignment with the positive choice to support your power.

YOU ARE LIMITLESS!

Give yourself permission!

If you're reading this book, chances are you're an adult. So it sounds odd to contemplate giving permission to yourself, right? But let's face it, we deny ourselves opportunity to experience aspects of life all the time. Whether it's a sweet treat, time to take care of yourself, or allowing yourself to DREAM BIG, we sometimes just need to know that it is okay to step outside of our box, believe we are worthy, prioritize ourselves first, learn our lesson, and feel the satisfaction.

Have FAITH!

Allowing yourself to dream big can be a scary endeavor. Not only are you declaring to the world (and more importantly to yourself) that you're worth it, you are also opening up some old issues around past failures, when you did dream and were let down. This brings up the big "V" energy: vulnerability. As we discussed in the science breakdown, our minds like to keep us safe, and being vulnerable is not safe! You are going to have to take a leap of faith. You are arming yourself with a new set of tools. These tools work within a language that your body and mind understand; they give you a strategic advantage and mitigate the level of risk you accept. Have faith in the system, and more importantly, have faith in yourself.

Understand Abundance:

We live in an abundant world. We have enough oxygen, water, and food. We have millions of cells in our body all working in perfect harmony. When I really grasped the concept of abundance, my world shifted. I have always had a fear of swimming in the ocean. On a particular clear day when the sun was sparkling on the sand below, I had mustered the courage to go out in the water with a friend. Upon our return toward shore, the waves shifted to a semi-rough chop and the water got murky. As I urgently stroked in and out of every trough, gasping for breath, I gathered the courage to look back beyond the next wave. Anticipating only the sight of a dark shadow, I was shocked to realize the enormity of the vast ocean. In that moment, I experienced a sudden connection to the water and its infinite expanse. I was absorbed in its movement and rhythm. I could sense the breadth of its reach from my shores all the way to the far reaches of the world. I felt the abundance of the experience. Abundance is everywhere. You just have to look.

When you find your abundance, you will find what you are entitled to receive in this universe.

Get ready to receive! You're worth it!

In our society we are taught that it is better to be a giver than a receiver. And while I agree in part, I think we often take the concept to the extreme. To realize our full energy potential, we have to allow ourselves to receive.

Use your manners!

Think of a conversation with a friend or acquaintance who constantly complains about almost anything; and despite countless hours of your faithful listening and advice, never seems to overcome the negative perspective. When you dream and set intentions, you send a message that you want to experience change. But if you aren't open to receiving what the universe wants to send back, you are in effect behaving no better than your friend! Even the scope of your wildest dreams is within reach in this realm. So with all due respect, find your manners, get out of your own way, and accept the good you have coming!

Expect the Unexpected

The more you focus on the energy of your dream the greater the probability of some aspect of it being fulfilled. When we expect the unexpected, there is significant room for anything to happen. So why limit yourself?

SUMMARY:

ATTRIBUTES OF DREAMS:

They rely on a charge of emotion and repetition of thought patterns to increase their strength or probability of manifestation.

They never manifest exactly how we envision them or in the timeframes we give them.

They don't have a physical attachment, but rather an energetic attachment. Focusing on the energetic aspects of the dream increases the charge and probability of recognizing the dream.

They don't exist in the future and are formed by our past. Therefore, the only time we recognize our dreams is in the present moment.

Kari Caldwell

To the extent that something or someone effects you is the extent that it's your opportunity to take a transformative action and free yourself from letting other people and situations make you something you're not!

—John Douillard, DC

Kari Caldwell

Strategy 3:

Own Your Story; Own Your Power

Purpose: Release Energy

What to Do with the Negative: Whose Story Is It Anyway?

How to: Body, Mind & Spirit

Strategy 3: Own Your Story

Own your story. Has anyone ever said this to you? Owning your story is a big deal and very important over your lifetime. I have plenty of friends and acquaintances who would definitely flinch if I told them about this concept. For many of us it can be incredibly painful to deal with our negative aspects. Many people prefer to ignore their story and, instead, focus on drinking, shopping, or other activities to numb the unhappiness, such as self-doubt, shame, guilt, frustration or feeling left out.

When we actually consider our story, it is easy to focus on peripheral reasons for the incongruences between the life we experience (our story) and our actual dreams. Maybe you had kids unexpectedly. Maybe you didn't want kids, but had them because you thought you should. Maybe your spouse's job (or lack of one) keeps you from recognizing your dreams. Maybe you are overweight. Maybe you have an illness.

There are a myriad of reasons we tell ourselves why we haven't gotten there. But at the end of the day, they are all stories. Our true story is one of abundance. Our true story exceeds all limitations and can be recognized regardless of experience.

Most people choose not to own their story. Admittedly, there are still aspects of my own story with which I have not yet dealt. And that is okay. That being said, the rewards for owning your story far exceed anything you can imagine. When I began the process of owning my story, I started with just listing my intentions--figuring out my dreams. But the more immersed I became in the intention-setting process, the clearer it became which pieces of my story I either did not like or no longer wanted to experience. And WOW! Does it feel good to tell yourself it is okay to let those things go. In fact, it is downright liberating! For example, social dynamics were always cumbersome for me. Because I people, I found myself entwined in many relationships that I could not balance. I worried needlessly about innuendos of conversations and their significance. Adding to my hours of deliberation was a focus on family members getting along at gatherings so that everyone was "happy." So many of these thoughts were really irrelevant given my specific intentions. Owning your story empowers you to control where your power aligns with intentions and where it doesn't. At least once you have this information, you can intentionally choose to continue to hand over your power or to seek a new path of aligning your thoughts and actions.

I encourage you as your read through this section to contemplate your own story. What are you ready to release? What do you know you should release but can't figure out how? Can you envision your life without a certain aspect? Just remember, your process all starts with baby steps!

CREATE ROOM FOR NEW

Our story provides the roadmap to where we hold our power and to where we have let it go. In reviewing our experiences, we begin to recognize a personal energetic landscape. When you consider your energetic story and the thoughts, ideas, beliefs, people, memories and emotions that make up your landscape, you gain an overall perspective of how well your journey aligns with what you set out to achieve.

This energetic perspective will help you navigate through your journey by providing insight into which choices or turns you have made that have compromised your power and steered you away from alignment with your intentions.

Do you need to experience more of some energies and fewer of others? Are there energies that you thought were part of your story, but upon review you don't recognize? For example, did you set out to experience relaxation, but found adventure instead? Focusing on our story helps us determine how we want to proceed.

Ownership of your personal energy is achieved through evaluating the illuminated energies and recognizing how they fit into your overall "map." Do your energies cause contraction and interfere with expansion? Or your ability to experience your journey? This evaluation also provides perspective of the energies you control: your emotions, thoughts, people and experiences. Choosing to look at these energies differently is the key to transforming the aspects of your story that are not in alignment with your desires. When you choose different thoughts, emotions, friends, and experiences, you redirect energies; and most critically, create room for new, positive, abundant energies. And you cause all of the energies to move and transform.

WHOSE STORY IS IT ANYWAY?

In evaluation of our story, it is significant to examine which aspects of it belong to us and which belong to others. When reviewing our landscape, is every memory, thought or idea from our journey our own? No, most likely not. As you attempt to describe your "landscape" to a friend, your overall impressions and stories will be full of other nuances you've picked up from other travelers along the way.

In life the "nuances" that impact our story are very significant. Consider present society's relationship with information. We are addicted to our TVs and phones, and depend on instant feedback and news. The internet and super technologies all ensure that we have ready and instant access to global events. Information connects us to the rest of the world in profound and meaningful ways. The expanse of knowledge available to us is amazing.

But our steady, habitual consumption of media events comes with a heavy price: it is very easy to lose track of what information and stories are truly ours versus those from outside, unreliable sources. In our consumer-driven culture, media and corporations and government know all too well how to take advantage of our thirst for excitement and desire to connect. Accordingly, they offer thoughts and ideas for our pleasure that are aligned with their agenda--not aligned with the greater good for you, the almighty consumer.

We are experiencing life faster than ever before. As the volume of information increases, the demand on our bodies to process, filter and file the information increases, and we run the risk of experiencing information overload. When a major event occurs, we get the information instantly--not at the five o'clock news or in the morning paper. As a result, we are forced to filter our thoughts, form an opinion, and respond faster. And while most people can decipher obvious agendas of corporate greed or political manipulation, the subtle side effects of needing to filter this barrage of information at such a fast pace increases our risk of consuming ideas that are not in alignment with our values. We dance a fine line between "knowing it all" and overloading our brains and triggering chronic stress and anxiety.

While pointing a finger at the media is easy, the reality is that our society as a whole is moving faster. We spend less time connecting. Families no longer spend time cooking and eating together; meals are available with the push of a button. Kids are encouraged to participate in many activities outside the home. To further compound our "connection" crisis, our means for communicating with each other has accelerated to unfathomable speeds; instead of writing a well thought out letter to a friend or loved one, we fire off text messages or "tweet" in forty words or less. In many ways, our life has gotten far more convenient, but with the convenience, we forego the repeated activities that connect us to our roots, our values, and the deep thought and pondering that comes with self-introspection.

YOUR TRUE POWER IS YOURS TO OWN

This self-introspection also helps us stay connected to our "true story." When we disconnect from our reality, we lose sight of what matters. And we lose the ability to control events and circumstance in our life.

Understanding the nature of our true power is critical to recognizing when and where we have released it. Our true story consists of love and abundance.

Abundance. We live in an abundant world; simply look outside and see nature's evidence. Experiencing abundance energetically means you experience infinite good. This supply may appear in the physical form as health, money, or freedom—essentially everything you need to experience a free and harmonious life.

Love. Love is the most powerful force we can experience. It is the creating and attracting energy that causes all of life to function. Our desire to live comes from a deep seated love for life. Without love we would not be drawn to what will support us.

Our true nature, therefore, is an abundance of love. The experience of love for ourselves and our life is the true seat of our power.

WHO HOLDS YOUR POWER?

Our energetic story consists of the energies that either support or detract from the experience of this love. Our story matters because it shows where we hold our power and where we don't. When we possess power we are stronger and more confident, especially with controlling our life and claiming the intentions that are rightfully ours.

Often we don't recognize when we have handed our power away. It is not something we intentionally set out to do, however, once we have done it, we set a precedent for the pattern of energy to flow.

After casting off our power, it is not always apparent if we still possess any of it or not. It may not be until you struggle to attain a goal that you begin to recognize the symptoms of having given it away. You may think you are doing something for all the right reasons, but, inevitably, you will not recognize your goal.

Unfortunately, when we establish a pattern of handing over our power, the pattern becomes very habitual. As a consequence, we begin to recognize the physical manifestation of it in our life.

Consider your relationship with food for a moment. Food is a nutrient, a source of fuel for our bodies. Yet, in our culture many people use food as a coping mechanism for managing stress, sadness, or other negative energies. (I discuss the energetic perspective on why in Strategy Four.) Food is not intended energetically to be a coping mechanism. If it were, we would be able to eat a pint of ice cream when we are depressed with no consequence. So when we choose food for coping, we contract the negative energy and don't allow it to flow. We essentially stop listening to our body, which does not need ice cream when in a positive energy mode. We disempower the natural flow of emotions. The point is we do not believe we can process the emotion on our own so we hand our power over to the energy of food. In an isolated circumstance, this is not a problem. But the more we utilize food to cope and contract the negativity, the more power we hand over to food and the more "blocked" the negative energy becomes. In effect, this creates an energy density in our bodies. Accordingly, our body will follow the direction from the energy around it. Not only will our body begin to crave and reinforce the "ice cream" habit on a chemical level, but also on a physical level with weight gain.

So ask yourself how many times a day do you go to the snack cabinet when you are hungry? And how many times do you do it just because you are mad, tired, bored or upset?

Money is another energy that can hold our power. Money in its true energetic form is nothing more than the energy of gratitude. Before currencies were invented, people would barter. Either work, labor, or goods would be exchanged for resources people were lacking. The farmer would bring grain from the fields in exchange for dry goods from the store or an animal. It was an equal exchange of efforts, a form of gratitude. Society created currency as a mechanism to create equality among the values of the resources. Still, it represented the resources and was given in gratitude for the exchange. It is probably fair to say, however, that we do not think of money as a symbol of gratitude any longer in our society. Money, now, typically conjures thoughts of greed, lack, and constriction. Remember Uncle Scrooge? In fact, money has so many negative connotations to it that we wonder how anyone maintains a healthy relationship with it. How is your relationship with money? Do you hand any of your power over to it?

If you worry about your bank account, you have handed your power over to money. If you worry about spending or in any way focus your beliefs around the concept of "lack," you have handed your power over to money. If you think you don't have enough, you have handed your power over to money.

And chances are, if you do experience an imbalance with any energy in your life, you have handed your power over to it in some capacity. So what causes us to cast off our power?

LIMITING BELIEFS

Limiting beliefs are the root cause of all loss of power. When we have learned perceptions, beliefs or ideas that are inaccurate, then we will engage in behavior and make choices according to this "inaccurate" information. This faulty information can be referred to as a limiting belief because it limits our ability to perceive our entire story or "landscape." It limits our ability to connect with our power.

Limiting beliefs are restrictive and can inadvertently cause contraction in our lives. Imagine setting out on your trip again, but this time you are going to utilize your personal map from your last trip. This map includes your best compilation of memories, events, people, and resources you will take along. But unbeknownst to you, it also includes "limiting beliefs." As you set out for your destination, you begin to recognize that the landscape appears slightly different. As you recall the details of the plan, you know there are certain crossroads you need to find, but the more you search, the more lost you find yourself. As you review your map, you begin to see that certain "turns" you made were not from your own experience, but from choices you made based on the advice of other travelers you had met along your journey.

We begin to learn limiting beliefs at a very young age. We file them away and store them to recall at a later date or in a time of need. While these "beliefs" are stored away, our "energy" story continues to evolve and transform. It is just like a computer, where technology advances at such a rapid rate that it can be outdated in months. This analogy is stunning because many of our responses to our environment are based on "limiting beliefs" or outdated information.

When our story contains outdated energies, whether from a belief in our childhood, or from a cultural system, society, or peer group, we find ourselves experiencing unnecessary stress and hardship. This hardship "blocks" energy by causing the energy to contract.

As observers of our own story, we are given the power to evaluate the "blocks" in our energy, and adjust our review of our landscape by re-directing the energies we wish to expand and experience.

OUTSIDE ENERGIES

We can all relate to the experience of energies outside of us; think of walking into a room and sensing tension. You did not experience the tension prior to walking into the room, yet there it is once you cross the threshold. Other easily identifiable outside energies are media and large groups that congregate, whether for religious, sports, or political reasons.

I want to draw your attention to the energies you experience that belong to other individuals. For example, think of a friend or co-worker who has been in a terrible mood. While her energy is outside of you, once she directs her negativity in your direction, it is "stuck" on you. You may not recognize it at the time, but later in the day, you may catch yourself exhibiting the same negative behavior.

These outside energies, by definition, are separate from ourselves. They come from a different source and are not a part of our normal energetic signature. And significantly, they are sticky. I often find it's easiest to imagine outside energies like a burr you might pick up in the woods. The burr will stick to a pant leg and travel with you until you deal with it. Like a burr, outside energies are a nuisance and can inflict pain. Generally, we know we are experiencing outside energies when we feel we are not being ourselves. We may realize, for example, that we have lost patience more quickly than normal.

Regarding these "traveling" energies, I am not saying that they are malicious or intentional. But the energies of anger, hatred, self-doubt, hostility, and spite are not in alignment with our nature. Yet, we may learn to harbor them through limiting beliefs and learned behavior. The longer we harbor them, the greater their physical impact becomes. For example, prolonged exposure to the energy of self-doubt will lead to depression, which we know is caused by chemical imbalances in the brain. In this case, our body is simply aligning with the negative energy.

When we objectify an energy, we remove the power these energies have over our personal identity. And we can better appreciate the profound impact they have on our experience of our true self. Ultimately, the goal is to reclaim your power over negativity and embody positivity. If your physical body has progressed far enough that you suffer from depression or other negative thought patterns, please seek medical assistance to help manage these energies. And apply this perspective to understand that negative energies do not define who you are or who you are meant to be. Empower yourself to embrace your true nature.

BODY, MIND & SPIRIT

How do we begin the evaluation of our energetic story?

First, we must become acquainted with the landscape in which our story lives: our body, mind, and spirit. Many of us perhaps are familiar with these concepts through religion or maybe from your Yoga class at the gym. Your ability to recognize where your energies live in your body is fundamental to correctly choosing the energies you wish to experience or inscribe in your energetic story.

Where energies live: body, mind, spirit:

Body: Think of a fear you have; consider snakes or spiders or a fear of heights and falling off a cliff. If presented with the fear, you may experience a feeling of sickness or paralysis or your skin crawling. This is your body's response to the fear. But what is your mind doing? If you are standing inside a high building looking down from inside the window, what is your mind's response? It does not hold the same belief that all heights are dangerous; thus you may attempt to look out the window to at least see what is out there. In this case, your "spirit" or the consciousness of your energy body, will probably assist your mind to help you appreciate the beautiful landscape.

Mind: The mind is tasked with being analytical. Data and facts are good examples of the types of information on which the mind places value and retains it. For example, the mind may retain a joke because it recognizes some humorous irony. The body and spirit are oblivious to this nugget of information that the mind has stored away. However, one night, while out with friends enjoying yourself, that joke "pops" into your head. The mind delivers the joke beyond expectation. It might cause an uproar of laughter so that your body "knows" the joke--it has responded physically with laughter. Your spirit also "knows" the joke, and has filed it away as a great mechanism for experiencing connection and bonding with friends.

Another example of a story that lives in the mind are the tales we create to give meaning or explanation of a situation. Consider friendship. A close girlfriend and I recently went through a period of time where we did not speak. Initially, it occurred because we were both exceptionally busy. But as time passed, we lost track and stopped prioritizing contact with each other. I caught myself making up stories about why she hadn't called or included me in certain activities. Because some time had elapsed, it was difficult to call each other and clarify. Finally, after recognizing the apparent sadness and loss of the friendship, I found appropriate words to share with her that did not assign fault to either of us for the hiatus. As it turns out, we both had been creating stories about the lack of communication. And while our friendship has transformed, our bond is still strong. Neither of us is experiencing the loss any longer, and we both can continue to support one another, despite the changes.

Spirit: There are things our spirit just knows. For example, think of a time when you have a "gut feeling," but your mind directs you to do something else. Sometimes we listen to our "spirit," and sometimes we don't. Spirit is your intuition or sixth sense. So think of a time when you really wanted something. Your mind just couldn't stop thinking about it. Maybe it's a bowl of ice cream. Your body is desperately craving that delicious, creamy delight. But your mind knows that it is probably the wrong choice. So what does your spirit believe? What does your spirit want fulfilled? That depends....

An instance of the spirit intervening pertains to an experience my mom had recently with my kids. She had just returned home from a visit to the town where she had spent her summers as a kid. Together with her brother, they had revisited an old ice cream shop that had served up all of their childhood favorite flavors and cones. She was enthusiastic about all their fun memories together. Thus when my kids came to visit her, she found herself relishing that same ice cream cone again. Her spirit was desperate to create the connection between her childhood and the moment she was enjoying with her grandchildren, and to create new ways for the memory of her childhood to carry into her present-day life. Now, when she chooses to have ice cream with my kids, it is forever linked to her wonderful memories from years ago.

OWN YOUR STORY

Control your own energies—and thus control the output of your story.

Step One: What energies are you experiencing in life? Could you use a little more laughter, a little more time, patience or love? Outline the energies you currently have. Compare them with the energies you identified in your intentions from the Dream Big section.

Step Two: Release what no longer serves you or is not in alignment with your energies from the Dream Big section. Releasing is critical for three reasons: 1) We cannot acquire or attract something new if we don't have "room" in our energetic space, and 2) Nature abhors a vacuum. When you eliminate an energy that no longer serves you, you immediately attract something new, and 3) You will continue to attract junk-- e.g., situations or energies--related to what you want to release, if you don't get rid of it.

Examples of Energies and Beliefs to release:

Energies: Which of your energies do you not need or care to experience any longer? Maybe it is a "friend" who only likes to talk about himself. Recognize this energy and set the intention to release it.

Beliefs: What limiting beliefs are you living with that are influencing your current circumstances? Are they your beliefs? Did you learn them from your parents? Your culture? Your friends or school? Limiting beliefs are more difficult to discover. But with practice you will begin to recognize them. For example, the concept of worthiness was one of my personal issues. I believe in the system of "earning" something based upon hard work. What I came to understand is that we don't necessarily "earn" everything; we are entitled to everything—our nature is having abundance. Therefore, we need to be open to receive it. All of the hard work in the world won't help us achieve something if somewhere in our belief structure (body, mind, and spirit) we believe we aren't worthy. I had to learn that in order to acquire something I needed my unfettered belief and subsequent actions to cause it to come into my life—not just rely on hard work alone.

Create new energies in your life:

Step One: Now that you've cleared the "space" in your energetic story, start to write the story....What energies did you identify from the Dream Big section? Begin to make choices that support these energies. Where can you start to recognize them? If love is one of your energies, do you simply "know" that you are meant to experience love? Can you find activities that will help you experience it? Maybe it isn't in the exact form you are looking for (e.g., intimate relationship), but you can find it in other areas of your life. For example, if you have a pet or a family member who is a favorite, focus on your love for them. Talk about it. Draw attention to it. Create the space for new "love."

Step Two: Whether owning your story is easy for you or if you aren't sure what to do, giving gratitude is the best way to discover and support the energies you want to experience. Reflect on what you are grateful for in your life. Honor it. Think about it regularly. And Pay Attention to it.

Making room for new energy helps you weave in aspects of the new energies you already have in order to attract a broader experience of these energies. Begin to recognize where support of new energies is in your life. Maybe new people begin to show up, or maybe circumstances that really used to bother you don't anymore. Continue to build on the little "shifts" and gradually you will notice more abundance.

SUMMARY:

ATTRIBUTES OF YOUR STORY

Stories are built by personal experience and observation.

Stories are not always our own. We acquire many aspects of other people's stories.

We experience our stories physically (health and emotions), in our mind (facts and ideas), and in our energy body or "spirit" (our intentions and desires).

Kari Caldwell

Act. Don't React.

-Unknown

Kari Caldwell

Strategy 4:

Fuel Your Energy Body

Purpose: Expand your Energy

What to Do with the Negative: No Excuses!

How to: Regenerative Energies

STRATEGY 4:
FUEL YOUR ENERGY BODY

Do you suffer from a chronic stress, an illness or disease? Perhaps not, and you are completely healthy. I know that I thought I had my whole health and told doctors that information. Migraines seemed to be the only issue. Bunches of tests always showed no obvious cause, so I relaxed and began to rely on my prevention medication. In fact, my drugs were so terrific that when I started running, they helped me drop numerous pounds in three months. Even after pregnancies, I found, weight loss—with the drugs--no problem! Healthy, skinny and happy!

This little formula seemed perfect until side effects started to present themselves. I began to notice a distinct correlation between taking my medication and a new cloudiness in my left eye. Of course when I looked up information on this drug, blindness was listed as a side effect. Although it seems outrageous and absurd to me now, I contemplated letting my eyesight go. When you know that without a drug you will get a devastating migraine, perhaps for two to three weeks straight, you get scared. My life would potentially cease to exist as I knew it. How could I ever cope with having to make such a decision?

I prayed for guidance. And in the midst of this contemplation, I found hope. My brother had recently done "energy" healing with a coach who was quite instrumental in helping him shift some energies so he could work more efficiently in his corporate world job. I had to jump on this opportunity.

In my first session we did a deep guided meditation that identified energies, and helped me move and adjust them. I did not know at the time if this work would be enough to feel results. Quite honestly, I just hoped it would help me manage the inevitable stress that I knew would ensue when a migraine cycle started. What I experienced in the subsequent weeks was not only "less stress," but also the all-important courage to transition from my medication. In hindsight, words do not adequately express the profound relief, gratitude, and hope with which I was filled in those initial sessions.

Miraculously, I was able to abandon the migraine drugs and experience few enough incidents to be encouraged in my new "energetic" direction. Initially, I was baffled by the impact simple "energy" work could have on a problem I had experienced for over half of my life. I began to recognize that the energies were acting as a form of "fuel" in my body. The more I worked with removing negative energies, and supporting positive ones, the better I felt. What I was essentially doing was learning to fill my body with the energy of love.

Interestingly, for a period of time energy medicine alone was enough. By the time my migraine cycles tried to increase, I had enough momentum to continue to fight and "get to the bottom" of what was causing them. Thus began my journey into the world of intentionally "fueling my body."

What I would come to recognize is that properly fueling our body, whether with food or energy, is the greatest and easiest form of self-love we can exercise. Literally, through intention and choice, we can love ourselves and reclaim our own powers.

REGENERATION

Our bodies live in a state of expansion and contraction. In the biology community these modes are called growth and protection. Growth is triggered when our body is in a state of abundance, and protection is triggered when there is a perceived threat to the organism. We relate to these states of being as feeling happy and healthy, or feeling ill with dis-ease (being sick) and experiencing stress.

The body's 50 trillion cells are incapable of experiencing both states simultaneously. In other words, the longer the stay in a protection mode, the more chronic your stress becomes and the fewer nutrients and vitality your cells receive. Thus if you remain in a state of chronic stress, your body will not continue to repair, regenerate and regrow.

Think of it this way: experiencing chronic stress is like remaining in an extended period of "fight or flight." Your body's protection mode cannot differentiate between being chased by a lion or receiving a negative email from your boss at work.

The relevance of each of these growth and protection states far exceeds the physical state alone. Prolonged experience of the protection mode on an energetic level has a cumulative effect on both the physical body and the energetic body. Energies experienced during a state of stress emit similar frequencies. Accordingly, our body becomes magnetized to attract people and circumstances to support these energies.

Regeneration. Regeneration, in physical terms, is the process of breaking down and rebuilding. Therefore, the key to applying the Energy Positive Perspective is to adjust our perspective to include energies of "regeneration." We do this by shifting our mental thought perspective from one of degeneration to regeneration. We begin the process by focusing on the regeneration that occurs in our body on a cellular level every moment. This subtle shift in attention facilitates the movement and transformation of negative energies ultimately prompting the energies of regeneration. These new energies trigger this same process on an energetic level by supporting our body's natural physical regeneration processes.

Think about it this way:

The American architect Louis Sullivan taught "...form ever follows function." If form follows function, then energy follows thought. If our thoughts reflect degenerative energies such as, "I am sick," "I don't have enough time," "My boss is a jerk," or "I will never get all of this work done," then the apparent supportive energies for those thoughts are anxiety, stress, worry, fear, disease, and frustration.

Unfortunately, our society and technologies "stack the deck" against us with constant and degenerative current events messages about our life situations. They focus on chatter about health care crises, the impending cold and flu season, murder rates, and war around the world. If, however, our thoughts went the opposite direction to include regenerative energies, such as, "I am healthy," "I am productive," or "I am relaxed," then we communicate the message of safety and growth to our body. To keep our bodies in a state of regeneration we need to first embody regenerative energies.

Managing Stress.

Also, understanding the physiological impact of stress can help you regulate or choose your responses and types of support needed, for example, healthy food, more water, or a good friend to listen. If you are in a prolonged state of stress, there are probably several physiological mechanisms going awry.

Our body is conditioned to ensure our survival. It will mount a response—no matter the trigger or perceived threat. So whether the belief relates to survival or simpler issues of safety is irrelevant. Our body cannot physiologically differentiate among its "stressors." Our job as the "user" is to navigate these complex programs within our human bio-computer, and effectively utilize its communication systems to further understand the intricate relationships between our body and the flow of energy through our system.

NO EXCUSES!

Thoughts, emotions and nutrients: Your daily food and self-care choices are not only critical regenerative energies, but are also easy to make. Your cells consume energy, which includes thoughts, emotions, and nutrients. There is no wrong choice when it comes to fueling your body; there are simply choices that either support growth or protection, regeneration or degeneration. Thus the more regenerative and higher quality energy going in, the better the output.

Choosing regenerative energies—no matter what:

The experience of prolonged negative emotions has the same effect as making bad food choices for yourself. Yet, for many different reasons, we continue to allow ourselves to experience negative emotions or self-limiting thoughts. If something feels bad, then skip it. Choose positive energies. If you are tired of experiencing a negative energy, such as stress or anxiety, then find a means to calm yourself—even if only momentarily. Exercise and meditation among other things are proven to increase endorphin levels and help reverse the side effects of stress.

Personally, though, I am acutely aware of how inaccessible and ineffective those "tools" can be when your circumstances don't allow for it. A friend of mine was given the advice to go for an early morning walk to reduce stress; but how did this fit into her current schedule of getting three to four hours of sleep a night with two babies under 18 months? Taking an early walk seemed highly improbable, so WHAT do we do to incorporate regenerative energies when we don't have the physical time or energy?

REGENERATIVE ENERGIES FUEL YOUR BODY

Step One: Set the Intention

Often when life turns upside down, we add more activities; we might think, "If I can only get to the gym today," or "I need to take a night class at school." Inevitably, however, we fail because our present circumstance is chaotic and overwhelming. My advice to you is: no matter what your negative circumstance entails, do NOT focus on adding activities. Rather, do what works within your present schedule and abilities.

Intention-setting creates the energy for improvement. Your first step is to create the energy to make space. This may mean telling yourself that you have the time (with a mantra) and can overlap one activity with another (such as doing a breathing exercise in the car).

Your intentions should include making adequate time for motivation, the right choices for your unique body, and a fulfilling, enjoyable experience available to you.

Step Two: Commit

Some health and wellness programs encourage making drastic changes, such as getting to the gym at five a.m., and gulping down the latest unpalatable concoction three times a day. While this approach works for some people, most of us struggle to recognize sustained success OR we never find happiness or fulfillment in following others' ideas along the path to our own fulfillment.

When you commit to your intentions, there is nothing short term about the success. Yes, depending on your intention and your unique body composition, a cleanse or detox could be in order. Exercise is always helpful, but the amounts and type are different for everyone. The intention you set is entirely unique to you. For example, if you don't enjoy walking or vigorous exercise, joining a gym will be a short term prospect—and when you stop following through, you will feel failure, thus not remaining committed to your intention. In this case, you need to start with what is attainable; maybe intentionally walking up and down your stairs a few times a day—and building from there.

Step three:

Determine the activities that will match your intentions and follow through with them: Food Choice, Self-Care, Meditation, Positive thoughts, water, breathing, and exercise. All of these positive energy expanding exercises are included in the Lifestyle section.

Step Four: Recognize the only permanent thing is change itself.

Your desires, food choices, and time all fluctuate and are the factors that feed your ability to support your body. The key to sustainable success is to fluctuate with them—and not lose focus on fulfilling the intention. For example, if you suddenly don't have time to get to the gym due to a schedule conflict, make adjustments in another area to compensate.

Most important, don't pressure yourself. Establish a bare minimum of activities in the beginning. Once you have accommodated these into your routine, add in more. Whether you seek improved health, reduced stress, better physical fitness, or simply to experience change, your continued support of your energy body will facilitate your desired transformation.

TYPES OF FUEL: THOUGHT FOR FOOD

The spectrum of energies available for us to experience is boundless. But the most powerful and transformative energies are love and gratitude.

Exploring the properties of water provides distinct insight into the relationship between our bodies and the energy around us:

Water is vital to life. Research shows that water comprises somewhere between 70% to 85% of a mature human body (statistic varies).

More importantly, water is considered to embody vitality. Victor Schauberger, researched the nature of water and found that in its natural state it "stores" information and frequencies and moves with a spiraling, vortex action. Dr. Masaru Emoto expanded upon this research to not only demonstrate water's vitality, but also its ability to exchange information with its environment. In his book, <u>Messages From Water</u>, Dr. Emoto froze samples of water from different sources and found significant discrepancies:

 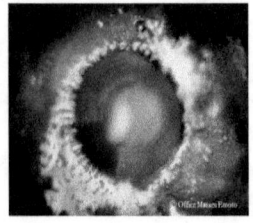

He found that crystals from spring water (left) were intricately formed and geometrical, while the crystals from polluted water were distorted.

Inspired, Dr. Emoto further established the exchange of information in the environment by playing music, writing words and utilizing thoughts to influence the water. The resulting water crystals revealed unique discrepancies depending upon the type of "frequency" to which the water was exposed. For example, when the words "hate," "kill," and "dirty," were taped to a vial of distilled water, distorted, globular looking water crystals were produced. In contrast the words "love," "gratitude," "thank you," and "friendship" produced spectacularly formed intricate crystals.

If the human body is comprised of at least 70% water, and the water within the human body can be influenced by the energies around it, then the quality of food and thought energies must be high to ensure and support health, beauty and regeneration. When we support our body with positive expansive energies, every aspect of our energy system responds.

PACE YOURSELF

When we consider working with energy, we are not going to experience drastic change overnight. For example, you can't expect to bench press 200 pounds the first time you lift weights. To achieve a newly formed goal, expectations must be adjusted to the tasks at hand. To reach the bench press goal, there are probably some fat cells that need burning, fibrous tissue to tone, and significant muscle strength to be built. Similarly, with energy you begin to build intentionally what you seek to experience.

The goal is to accomplish feeling and thinking energetically, while doing other things, such as driving the car, just breathing, or talking on the phone. Recognize that these smaller activities are enough as long as you recognize and experience progress.

FOOD IS LOVE

Do you have a poor relationship with food? Even if you answer "no," consider how many times you may have felt guilty about eating unhealthy food or too much of something. Food is a source of nourishment both physically and energetically, and it has strong ties to the energies of safety, support, laughter and love. If your grandmother baked bread, like mine, there's a high probability the smell of it baking and the taste of a warm slice with butter is hard to pass up. When food has positive energetic ties associated with it, you experience those energies and memories.

A common problem today, however, is that we don't discriminate well enough among the energies. When we lack the energies of love or self-love, we try to fill the void with an outside source, such as a grandmother's homemade bread, without doing the "work" to fill in the void with love from its true source. As a consequence, we give ourselves a "quick shot in the arm," followed by a "chaser" of self-loathing, guilt and general negativity.

A friend of mine was recently diagnosed with breast cancer. She received her diagnosis shortly after giving birth to her third child. Additionally, she works full time, and receives minimal support from her husband with household duties. Needless to say, she was experiencing a shortage of "love" energy.

Amazingly, upon learning of her diagnosis, her community stepped up and delivered enough food to support her family for months. Most of these caring contributions, however, were sweets and treats and some starchy pasta dishes. She was afraid to eat them because she knew she should be eating far healthier choices. On the other hand, she had to consider this specific situation: She was exhausted, stressed and short on love, and her friends had devoted much effort and care into preparation and delivery of the food. These dishes came from love, and her body needed love.

Drawing awareness to this amazing in-flow of caring and support helped her transition through a very challenging period of her life. We created a plan that helped her achieve balance by incorporating both the love food and some green alternatives, so that she was not in a position of having to reject what others had made for her.

SUMMARY:

ATTRIBUTES OF FUEL:

Making changes in your physical body, such as food choice, will trigger changes in your energetic body. Conversely, changes in your energy body will also trigger changes in your physical body.

All emotions are equal. There is no wrong or right emotion. The key is to keep them flowing. When they stop flowing, we experience symptoms of stress and anxiety.

You never stop fueling your body; every thought, emotion, and nutrient counts. There is no wrong choice, only choices that either support growth or protection.

Your beliefs become your thoughts,

Your thoughts become your words,

Your words become your actions,

Your actions become your habits,

Your habits become your values,

Your values become your destiny.

--Mahatma Ghandi

Kari Caldwell

Strategy 5:

Practice, Practice, Practice

Purpose: Build Your Energy Assets and Achieve Balance

What to Do with the Negative: Polar Opposites

How to: Integration

STRATEGY FIVE:
PRACTICE, PRACTICE, PRACTICE

Have you ever known what you want, and just can't wait to get it? The anticipation is intense, and we feel we HAVE to have it right now. The same desire applies to energy. Once I was completely clear on what I wanted and I could see the path before me, it took everything in my power to accept that it might not happen right then and there. The idea that good health, happiness, love, and laughter were all right at my fingertips was tantalizing! I could not release enough negative energies fast enough. And I could not practice enough positive energies fast enough. I wanted my path to be shown to me right then. I was fired up, feeling good, and ready to go!

Energy doesn't always work that fast though. To build energies requires repetition, commitment and patience. Ultimately, you are learning an energetic dance. There is give and take, momentum and withdrawal. When working with energy, a big awareness will come. This awareness will rock your world, literally, in a very positive way. You hit new plateaus and break glass ceilings. But with every new positive experience, there are other energies around you that must adjust to your "energetic change."

Additionally, when you reclaim personal power, you create a shift. Energies around you will need to adjust; this includes people and relationships. Think about it. If you've handed over power for a period of time, and then you start to reclaim it, the change will interrupt the flow and pattern of things. For example, a common example many of us can relate to is if you have typically hosted a family holiday meal, but want to stop the tradition. You have to choose to reclaim the time for yourself, and delicately work through the repercussions. While your choice may not be popular with everyone, you have to stick with your decision. In order to maintain a positive outlook and ride out these moments of energetic re-balancing, you have to reaffirm your commitment to retaining your power.

Ultimately, your practice is what gives you faith and confidence that you have taken the right path. It provides the foundation of strength we need to sustain our decisions and move the negativity to transition fully into the positive realm.

BUILD YOUR ASSETS

The more we own our power the more we build our energetic assets and experience their positive benefits. But like anything in life, it requires significant practice, repetition and dedication.

Energetic Assets are our personal Energetic Signature. We build energetic assets by focusing on a particular energy we desire. Recall the Energetic Signature from Perspective Four, "Flowing electrons produce a magnetic field, and spinning magnets cause an electric current to flow. Electromagnetism is the interaction of these two important forces. Combined, these forces make up vortices of energy or an energetic signature."

Think of it this way: In order to build energetic assets we essentially focus on intention (the flowing electrons that make a magnetic field) and action (the spinning magnets that make electricity) to strengthen and build the desired energies in our life.

MANIFESTATION: FROM AN IDEA INTO THE PHSYICAL WORLD

Before we focus on how to build our energetic assets, it is imperative to understand the process in which energy appears or manifests.

Body, Mind and Spirit—AND Environment.

Spirit. Energy begins as an intention. In Dream Big, we learned that our intentions are a form of energy within the field of intelligence that is seeking to manifest itself through us. Therefore, every idea we experience is a seed in our mind of those intentions.

Mind. Once our mind has translated the intention into an idea or thought, there is a physiological reaction that occurs, which translates the idea into the physical realm. Consider what you learned in science class about your nerve cells: If you want to scratch an itch, your brain says, "I need to scratch my arm," and then "sparks" or creates an impulse of light that triggers molecules to release and exchange information until the message reaches the intended receiver--in this case your hand.

Body. Once the message reaches the intended receiver there is a physical response and your hand reaches over to scratch your arm.

Environment. This is a very simple example of the process of an idea transforming from energy into a physical experience. When we consider more complicated energies of love, abundance and money, the process remains the same; however, there are more energies interacting (and interfering), and the process by which we experience these energies becomes more complicated.

When these more complex energies converge, however, we witness the energies of our intentions in the environment around us.

A CONVERSATION WITH ENERGY

Often when we think of building something, we think of hard work, physical effort, and repetition. We focus on the outcome. For example, if the desire is to build strength, we will go to the gym, exercise and eat well. Building energy assets requires this same effort. It requires we give our best effort. But there is one other attribute that is often overlooked: receiving.

Receiving is a critical component of working with energy. Energy is alive. It is intelligent, and it can be full of gifts and wonder. We must learn to dialogue with energy to fully appreciate what it has to offer.

Think of it this way: Working with energy is like having a conversation. You must be willing to do your part—share your perspective, but also listen. In our current state in our technological society, we are not good listeners. We spend most of our time instantly responding to messages. Only in the critical moments, such as a birth or death or illness, do we seem to give pause and listen to the information being given to us, and appreciate the "miracles of life."

LISTENING TO ENERGY

Body, Mind and Spirit.

Body. We are all familiar with the means in which our bodies speak to us. Whether we experience a general tired feeling, or a hunger pain, or a severe ache, we know these are cues by which our body speaks to us.

Often, they serve as a clue or indication of underlying problematic energies. For example, irritable bowel symptom is directly related to stress. In this case the physical symptoms of upset stomach are telling you, "Stop! Reduce stress now!"

The energies in our body also speak to us on a much more subtle level. Imagine a fear. If you actually visualize yourself experiencing your fear, chances are you felt that fear in your chest also. This is energy speaking in your body.

Mind. Our mind speaking to us is evidence. As you read these words, your mind is speaking. Our mind's job is to analyze and evaluate. It is literally hard-wired to perform this function in order to ensure our survival. When we experience stress, we feel the sensation of our mind racing because the mind, alone, cannot determine the best solution.

Often the issue with the mind is not whether or not we can hear it, but how do we get it to Stop! If you've ever tried meditation and can't get your mind to quiet down, then you can relate to this sensation. You may also think of your mind in overdrive, when you try to fall asleep at night and experience it racing.

The best bet to calm your mind is to intentionally invite it to co-create with you. When the mind is given permission to co-create, it slows down. Instead of just looking for solutions stored in your "bio-logical" database, the mind becomes a silent observer to the energetic environment around it, and begins to listen and hear options from an outside source, whether it is your body or spirit.

Sometimes the mind does not want to comply with the request to co-create and must be coerced. If you've ever been relaxing and then felt a sudden flurry of concerns come flooding forth, you can relate. Simply thank your mind and quiet it again.

Spirit. Whether we realize it or not, we are constantly receiving messages from the energy around us. Common examples of messages we receive are felt in the well-known "gut" feeling. This is your intuition, which can be an intense emotion, such as excitement in a crowded sports arena, or when you walk onto a stage to speak to a large crowd.

The more subtle ways energy can send messages is through people, ironies, and coincidences. Whether someone shows up right when you need her, or you "stumble upon" an old note from a friend and he happens to call you that afternoon, you are receiving messages from energy.

We benefit from the effort that artists, musicians, writers, and poets put into translating the world we see around us.

POLAR OPPOSITES:

There is always some form of communication there for us. The nature of energy is always polar: the positive does not exist without the negative, the light does not exist without the dark, and the good is not there without the bad. In fact, Newton's third law of physics states, "For every action, there is an equal and opposite reaction."

When you recognize that the nature of your

experience of energy is like a pendulum seeking balance, you become a better listener and observer; we open ourselves up to the ever fluctuating dance to create balance. When you experience a negative emotion or circumstance, there will always be a counter-balance that occurs energetically. We may refer to this counter balance as the "light at the end of the tunnel." When you struggle to find that light, have faith that the positive is coming; remain in a state of receiving and allow for the negative emotion to flow.

The best practice for removing negative energies is to practice silence. Silence empowers us to observe at what point in the swing the energies are. Upon observing, you can best determine whether you need to set a boundary so the energies don't repeat a swing back; or if you simply need to experience the energy so that it can flow and transform.

INTEGRATION

The goal of strengthening your energetic assets is to combine the energies you are seeking with those energies you currently experience to create a whole—or to integrate them. When we integrate energies, we are choosing to create space and actively make choices to transform our energy body into the overall energetic experience we desire.

Imagine that your energy body is like a basket. Or, as we described earlier, the proverbial toolbox. We start out in life with the basic seeds—our intentions. As we experience life, we fill our basket or toolbox with experiences of our intentions, and our observations of other people pursuing their own intentions. Depending on our circumstance, we can hand our seeds over to other people, or we can try to use their seeds. (We might think of this as living a life for someone else, not ourselves.) We may also get holes in our baskets that allow our "seeds" to drain out. (This occurs when we "hand" our power over to another person or limiting belief.) In order to build our energetic assets, we must first plug the basket's holes. Once the basket is secure, we are ready to start choosing the quality and type of seeds (or energies) with which to fill our container. It requires finding balance between action and inaction: first, planting and sowing the seeds, then cleaning out old rotten seeds, and lastly, waiting for the harvest to come in order to reap the rewards and fill our baskets again.

If our container is full, or if we do not have an adequate sized one, we will not retain the energy we seek to experience. Consider money energy: People dream of experiencing an abundance of money. Yet, often when people win the lottery, they are back to their former wealth within five years. This occurs because the basket, or their capacity for holding an abundance of money energy, was limited. Whether they spent it all, donated it, or gave to family, all actions became sources of holes, and an overflow of energy.

BALANCE

Our baskets and toolboxes are always full of both positive and negative energies. Energy does not discriminate. There are as many aspects to the energies available for us to build into assets as there are colors in the spectrum of the rainbow. Every emotion and energy presents itself at some point in our lives. Therefore, in order to sufficiently build energies, we must first strike a balance between both positive and negative energies.

This balance requires an intricate dance between doing and being. Too much of one thing and not enough of another or being overextended in the wrong direction, will cause stress. Balance is achieved by cutting back on doing and focusing on how you are supported.

ACTION & INACTION; GIVING & RECIEVING

Receiving is so much more than simply getting gifts on birthdays and holidays. Receiving can be in the form of a compliment or well wishes.

But does the thought of receiving make you uncomfortable? Do you automatically feel obligated to return the compliment, favor, or gift upon receipt? Unfortunately, our society teaches us that "it's better to give than receive." Our focus then becomes giving energy *out* instead of drawing energy *in*. This focus on giving halts the balanced flow of energy between giving and receiving.

Practicing receiving not only the positive gifts of nature and love, but also the negative energies, is critical to keeping energy flowing and ultimately building the energies for your basket.

Step One: Learn to receive. Practicing to receive is a difficult task for many people. Our society conditions us to give, give, give. But when we receive, we reinforce the energy of giving and taking. Receiving is the "polite" end of the conversation.

Step Two: Learn to give what you want to get back. If you want to get back negativity, then project negativity. If you want positivity, then project and choose positive action.

Step Three: Trust your gut. If you aren't certain about a situation, follow your instinct.

Step Four: Ask about your intuition. Check in with your body, check in with your mind, and check in with your spirit/energy body. How does what you are considering feel when you "ask" your body?

Step Five: Always seek balance. While you may not know how to process or respond to an energy, you can look for the balance instead of just responding with your habitual reply.

Step Six: Just say No. Practice controlling your energies by selecting which energies you put in your basket or toolbox. Often I have to tell my kids when they experience a negative energy to simply stop! While some self-pity, guilt, and frustration are natural and acceptable, there are limits. I will give my kids a time limit and then we work together to find an alternative, positive energy or emotion to experience.

Step Seven: Practice gratitude and kindness. Gratitude and Kindness are two of the most magnetic, transformative energies. These energies can literally transform the toughest situation into meaningful and profound experiences. Be grateful for everything you have, and you will receive more things for which to be grateful. Be kind in the face of meanness and your heart will fill with compassion and love. And you will attract more kindness, compassion and love into your life.

Step Eight: Look for the dialogue. Notice when you are acting and then experiencing an energetic "reaction."

Step Nine: Practice choosing multiple times per day something different and random. Then look for changes in your daily experience. Maybe people notice you look different or have more vibrancy or focus. At first it is a fun game, but then it compounds into a permanent status.

Step Ten: Always look for the gift, like a nugget of information, a beautiful sunset scene, or a series of songs that fit your mood perfectly. There is always a gift waiting for us around every corner. Our job is to look for it.

Step Eleven: Sit in silence in order to listen and observe, especially if you are trying to break a pattern of behavior. It is the best, most effective and fastest way to stop an energy dead in its tracks. You essentially stop the pendulum from swinging.

Step Twelve: The practice is in the details. Like anything, it starts with little steps. Practice the energies you desire on yourself first. Feel gratitude for a good night's sleep, for a great workout, for eating well, for brushing your teeth. The more you practice positive energies, the more love you will experience and the more you will receive positive energies in return.

SUMMARY:

ATTRIBUTES OF PRACTICE:

Before we recognize energies in our environment they must first integrate on the three levels of body, mind, and spirit.

Kari Caldwell

MIRACLES START TO HAPPEN WHEN YOU GIVE AS MUCH ENERGY TO YOUR DREAMS AS YOU DO TO YOUR FEARS.

–Unknown

Kari Caldwell

Strategy 6:

Expect Miracles

Purpose: Receive positive energy, receive miracles

What to Do with the Negative: Channel Chaos

How to: Synchronicity

STRATEGY SIX: EXPECT MIRACLES

My miracle occurred, oddly enough, in a church parking lot. In order to appreciate the significance of this moment, you have to know I hadn't been to church for some time. As an avid outdoor person, I generally preferred my communing and enlightenment to be among nature's finest sights and sounds, like in a woods or on a beach.

How I ended up in this church parking lot, I cannot say as I don't recall. I have blocked most of the trauma leading up to the moment. But what I distinctly remember was having a very explicit conversation with God. While everything in my life from the outside appeared to be great and normal, I was actually feeling somewhat desperate. Sure, we had moved three times in three years and had lost the same house twice. But I always had a roof over my head and healthy babies and a loving and supportive family. So this visit wasn't about any recent events, but more about a sensation of losing something of my inner self. I felt I might be changing somehow, and that thought felt confusing and scary. How could I return to "normal"? When you experience stress as I had, through having children and undergoing major life-changing events, many profound adjustments are needed and they impact how you perceive your own self. Perhaps the best explanation is to say you don't feel grounded in reality. You tend to go through motions without the usual, reliable commitment.

When you reach this point, you begin to wonder how many more stressors might have even a worse impact. That day I found myself in the parking lot I felt like I had encountered another stressor that perhaps I couldn't handle. I was struck by the profound realization that the foundation of my life, while based on all the right things--love, hard work, and ambition--had inherent flaws in it. The problem was I couldn't identify these flaws. I would later come to recognize that in incremental phases, out of a desire to please everyone around me, I had unavoidably handed all of my power to everyone else and kept none for myself.

On that miraculous day, I reached my crossroads. While I knew my family relationships ultimately would not change, I felt very stuck, as the realization of having no power was overwhelming. And I didn't have a clue as to how to get it all back so I could feel balanced and centered again. In my prayer I made it very clear that I wanted my family. I wanted my life and I wanted to experience love and success and fulfillment. I did Not want the grief, desperation, shame, and hopelessness that defined my present moment. I prayed that I would be strong enough to transform my circumstances, yet retain the wonderful support from my family. We can never predict what our future will hold for us or which people we will encounter on our path. Nor can we imagine the amount of time required or experiences needed prior to discovering that for which we are searching. At this critical time, I didn't know what resources would show up for me—or even that resources would show up.

But, now, I can tell you that every single resource I needed did materialize. And every single thing I asked for that day I have received--and then some. We often think of miracles as instantaneous and beyond comprehension, but they can also occur in small amounts over an extended period of time. They can be simple answers to a prayer for hope, faith and love, and for a deeper connection. That day I asked for everything I was lost, didn't have any plan, and felt I had failed at being successful. But the beginning of my miracle occurred because I believed I had to release my expectation and my control over the outcome. I was willing to let go and allow the magnificent force around us, whether it be God, the universe, or the divine, to lead the way. I recognized the power of this force and its ability to supersede any of our greatest efforts or wisdom.

In my life now I embrace at least one miracle every day. It may be small or seemingly insignificant to others, but for me these miracles are the sign posts that I am on the right path. They are one cohesive part of all the greater miracles I have been blessed to witness. We must find our own unique significance and meaning of our experience of life. We must step outside of our self-absorbed and naïve thought patterns to recognize the continual flow of this divine intelligence around us. When we incorporate the expectation of miracles into our lives, they become a daily and habitual experience.

EXPECT MIRACLES

Recall the quantum perspective. Within the field of energy, quantum particles take all paths—not just a singular, observed, if-then, path. In other words, it is simply our conditioned observations and expectations that significantly increase the probability of an energy "manifesting" or occurring in an expected manner. To restate, of all the (infinitely) possible ways energy can collapse (or appear) from the field of intelligence, the probability of energy collapsing in the manner we expect is significantly greater because of our expectation. When we remove our expectations, however, we increase the likelihood for the energy to collapse (or appear) from the field of intelligence in a welcome and unexpected manner. Therefore, according to the Energetic Perspective, the key is to release our control, and empower this field of intelligence to work its magic.

EXPECT THE UNEXPECTED

A miracle, which is what occurs when highly improbable or extraordinary events take place, can be experienced via thoughts, developments, or accomplishments in an unpredictable manner. It has greater significance and ability to occur when we take action to increase the probability of it happening.

To experience greater, more expansive positive energies, and to find true success through the fulfillment of our intentions, we must learn to increase the probability for miracles occurring in our lives. We do this by embracing the field of energy or intelligence from which miracles come, and by learning to expect them in our life.

Ironically, expecting miracles means that you expect positive *unexpected* events. When we anticipate the occurrence of unexpected, improbable events, we inherently release control of our expected outcome. In releasing the need to control the outcome, and expecting the improbable to occur, we open the door to strengthening the energy of improbable events unfolding.

MIRACLES ARE UNIQUE UNTO YOU

Improbable events, by nature, do not occur in linear order. Your job as an observer is to be the detective and interpreter of the randomness to create your own significance.

In turn, your desire and ability to link the significance of improbable events to your personal experience, further increases the future likelihood of experiencing more and greater improbable occurrences.

FIND THE FORCE WITHIN YOU

Identify miracles within you. When we draw our attention to who is doing the observing of the improbable events, we create a slight shift in our perspective. To fully understand this shift, consider the lessons of the Energy Positive Perspective:

Our body is experiencing atoms colliding together due to the force of gravity that creates the solid mass beneath us; the result is we see a solid chair in the room. Our skin feels hot or cold within the environment, and our eyes sense the variations of light as they scan the different symbols on this page.

To observe these processes we become aware that our sensory organs are functioning cohesively as one synchronistic unit. Our nerve endings are sending the messages to our brain, which is processing and prioritizing the information it receives. At this moment your brain is translating messages from linguistically structured "thoughts," and analyzing and comparing the information with similar previously stored data.

But consider for a moment who or what is orchestrating all of this activity. If your mind is busy analyzing, processing, and translating, then who is actually observing and experiencing?

The source that observes and experiences is your energy body. Your combined "vortices" of energy that create your soul is the same source of energy that creates miracles. In other words, the very foundation of our nature comprises the same energy that creates miracles and contains infinite intelligence. We simply translate this intelligence through our limited resource of the mind. Think of standing in a dark room. Our minds give us a flashlight to glance around the space. Empowering the observer within is like turning all of the lights on at full power.

SYNCHRONICITY:

Our ability to "sync" up with the energy around us is the first step to turning the lights on and creating miracles. In recognizing the energy flowing within us, we are able to recognize the energy flowing around us, which we refer to as synchronicity:

Synchronicity is a concept first explained by psychiatrist Carl Jung, which holds that events are "meaningful coincidences" if they occur with no casual relationship. (Tarnas, 2006)

In its simplest form, synchronicity is the "flow" or movement of nature.

How is it that thousands of birds can fly in intricate, complicated formations without ever colliding? How is it that thousands of fish can swim in perfect sync at high rates of speed? How does the flower bloom or the tree bear fruit?

We are an integral part of this energetic dance also. Our bodies have evolved according to the flow and timing of the energies available to us. Consider the springtime when you typically feel compelled to experience something new or re-organized. In the summer heat nature provides foods such as peaches and watermelons to provide nutrients that support the cooling mechanisms within our bodies. In the fall we find foods like nuts and squash to help us endure the winter cold.

Synchronistic events are not unrelated. There is a rhythm and a flow to life that is evident, and it orchestrates the very nature of our existence. The flow is evidence of the field of intelligence. It drives everything from our simple thoughts to the complex mysteries of the cosmos. Our ability to access this flow of energy and "sync" up with its inherent intelligence determines not only the level of support we receive from our environment, but also our ability to connect and access the realm of infinite possibilities.

These seemingly linear examples of synchronicity in our life explicitly draw attention to the rhythm in which we participate and from which we receive support. This support is not only critical to our survival but also invaluable when we are experiencing duress, loss or grief. We can increase the flow of this support by simply looking for it and intending for more of these energies to appear.

THE LANGUAGE OF THE UNIVERSE

The synchronistic flow of energy in the universe is often referred to as "The Language of the Universe." This language reflects the inherent give and take and transfer of energy and information that occurs—in our case, specifically between us and our environment. We focused on the activities of giving and receiving and action and inaction in Strategy Five as one means for engaging with the language of the universe. But there are other more direct ways to interact with the ever surrounding synchronistic flow of energy.

To recognize energy flowing in yourself it is necessary to draw your attention—as the observer--to where and how you observe this flow of energy and information.

Coincidence. The most common form of synchronicity that we observe is coincidence. To experience coincidence means that a remarkable concurrence of events occurs without a seemingly plausible connection. In other words, when coincidence occurs, it is merely an increased likelihood of improbable events coming together, which we refer to as miracles.

INCREASE YOUR OBSERVATION OF COINCIDENCE AND SYNCHRONICITY

The objective of "syncing up" with your environment is to amplify whatever degree to which you presently experience energy. Every moment of every day and with every breath we take, we are in sync to varying degrees with energy around us. In order to experience greater occurrence of coincidence and miracles, we simply need to observe it, appreciate it, and express gratitude for it.

We recognize synchronicity in seemingly significant and insignificant events. It could appear as repetition of experiences, thoughts, people, or emotions. You may recognize it initially in numbers that repeat or songs that play frequently or remind you of something you have been thinking about earlier in the day.

Coincidence can also show up where we are not looking for it:

I had a client who was experiencing a significant amount of stress and irritability at the end of summer. In Chinese medicine, our body needs to begin cooling the heat from the warmer months. Good cooling or natural transition foods at that time of year are watermelon and peaches. I suggested incorporating these foods into her diet; ironically, however, she had just purchased peaches at the store. When I asked her why she said they just looked delicious. But how much more was occurring? She would have never guessed that her energy knew it needed the peaches for support, and had sent the message to her body to crave the peaches.

Synchronicity can also show up in seemingly unexpected, random occurrences:

Shortly after becoming aware of the concept of synchronicity, I started to recognize front row and prime parking spaces were frequently available to me. At first I thought it was a fluke. (Parking spots are easy to manifest because a front spot is something you may want, but to which you have no emotional attachment.) But then I realized that it did not matter what the circumstance; they were always there, and not just at the grocery store. When going to a show one night with friends at a small venue, we were late and found the parking lot full. As we circled, I got a feeling we should look at the improbable location by the front door. Of course, there was our spot waiting for us. The best part, however, was that when leaving we were right in front of the bus, and able to meet one of my favorite bands!

There are also times when synchronicity and miracles show up no matter what, especially when we really release the outcome.

I've enjoyed applying this perspective to my own life. It is easy to practice with things in which we do not have a huge emotional investment, like a trip. When I travel, inevitably something will go awry. Whether minor or significant, I ground myself in the knowledge that something better is just around the corner. If a rental car or hotel room isn't available, I look at the situation from an energetic perspective and may find the energy is just arranging for a very nice upgrade.

Recently I enjoyed such an unexpected occurrence: I was driving my son to a karate tournament in which his participation was a last minute decision. As I began to search for a hotel near our destination, I found everything within many miles was full. In an effort to increase my search capacity (while driving), I enlisted my mom's help from home. She found a reservation and gave me the exit number, pointing out that the next exit beyond was well over 50 miles away. It was getting later and imperative I find this exit for the motel we had located. How in the world I drove right by it I will never understand, but I completely missed it.

Luckily, my mom hung in there with this bad news and helped me re-assess: it was better to continue in the wrong direction than to turn around. I would have to make up the lost time in the early morning. Now heading this way, we also had to go through a big city; luckily, Hot Wire came to the rescue with an amazing five-star room. From despair of the wrong turn, we quickly changed our attitude and became appreciative for having not just any lodging, but great lodging. We hit the pool for a relaxing swim and late dinner poolside. Within minutes a strange text appeared on my phone—it was from an old high school friend with whom I hadn't had contact in years. He and his family—with kids my son's age—had just driven 2,000 miles and checked into a hotel for the night. He had thought of me since they were now in my home state. As soon as he uttered those words, I asked, "Where?" First he said the city where we were, and then he gave the hotel name, which was, incredibly, right next door to us. How phenomenal! What an amazing visit we had!

Over the course of four hours, my son and I had gone from a completely chaotic situation to finding an amazing and unpredictable event! We, essentially, had channeled the chaos to create a positive, improbable outcome!

CHANNELING CHAOS

Chaos is the true nature of energy in the universe. According to the quantum, energetic perspective, *chaos* is the formless matter supposed to have existed before the creation of the universe. Thus, we bring order to the chaos around us through our observation of energy and our intention to interact with it. Our desire to observe, in turn, creates connection to the divine and exceptional forces. Our creative minds are what empower us to observe by channeling the chaos. By simply applying our will and intention, we invoke our imaginative and inspired energies to bring new order, and transcend traditional ideas, rules, patterns, and relationships. For example, works of art intend to help us connect to and interpret the meaning of the chaos. Art, then, is one means by which we can join or attach to the divine and exceptional realm.

Ironically, chaos is rarely considered a positive attribute or energy. This negative association stems from relationships with people who we have labeled chaotic. We describe them as being perhaps "out of control, weird, unpredictable, or unreliable." Most people struggle to maintain a lasting relationship with a chaotic personality for the long term.

Interestingly, we often recognize these characteristics in people who have depression or mental illness, or have been traumatized. In these circumstances their ability to connect or channel their creative thoughts to observe the divine realm is compromised.

Imagine you are interacting with a group of unruly teenagers or a family member who suffers from depression or is an alcoholic or bi-polar. The result is your ability to control the situation is limited. Chaos is unpleasant since there are usually many signals going in many directions at once, and identifying how to control them is frustrating.

Consider, however, an opposite reaction. Instead of focusing on the negative, unpleasant aspects presenting themselves in your tenuous circumstance, shift your perspective to be more positive. This can be very difficult to do as, generally, in the moment we are too consumed with "feeling chaotic" to recognize any positive aspects. But in the energetic world, the more chaotic and random a situation, the greater the likelihood of an improbable, positive event.

How can this be true? Because we are able and willing to release control and focus exclusively on the intended emotions. When we commit to those actions, we channel the chaos and ask for the improbable events, which can effect a positive outcome. Managing chaos is challenging, however, because trying to "feel good" in a "bad situation" takes extreme focus.

To overcome this discrepancy between experience and emotion we need to access our creative and imaginative energies. These energies are the key to manifesting the miracles we seek and to discovering the greatest solutions to our problems.

While greater solutions don't always appear on the timeline we set, the repeated process of imagining a positive, outrageous solution and choosing positive energies to support it will increase the probability of bringing order to your chaos.

This repeated process of first imagining and then experiencing, even if gradual at first, is the basis of our faith.

Energy is remarkable. The more open we are to experiencing it, the greater the probability of witnessing fascinating—if not miraculous-- occurrences. That is not to say you will understand them, but it is possible to witness them. And when you do, you just have to accept and appreciate that you have, indeed, seen a real miracle occur. Once such incident occurred shortly after I began to explore energy. And to this day, I have no idea how it happened, but it did. A dear friend of mine received that tragic call that every parent dreads--her daughter had just been killed instantly in a car accident. I had met her daughter in years past, and at some point we had exchanged phone numbers. But I had long since lost touch with her as our paths went separate ways.

Shortly after the call I met my friend and spent a long, excruciating day consoling her until family arrived to support her through the night. The following day I planned to see her in the evening. In the busy hours preceding our get-together, I saw that I had a missed call on my cell phone. As I looked closer, I saw the daughter's name and number at the top of my call list. Very confused and worried, I called the number. Could it be that my friend had retrieved her daughter's phone, and was calling me? But the computer on the end of the line said the number was "not in service."

Panicked, and really confused now, I drove straight to my friend's home, and showed her the incoming call on my phone. After comparing numbers, we both realized her daughter had not had that phone number or phone in over five years. (And, we learned in a follow up call to the carrier service that the number had not been recycled to another customer.)

We can all draw our own conclusions about how my phone managed to receive a call from someone who not only hadn't dialed my number in years, but no longer possessed the phone that called me, and had also just passed away. In the days, months and years since this call, I have never forgotten it. While at first a little "freaked" by its strangeness, both my friend and I have come to accept it as a wondrous miracle of final communication from her daughter. There is no other explanation.

Up until this phone call incident, logic and order ruled my world; but I have had to accept that quantum physics and the energetic perspective is the only viable explanation: In the midst of my friend's supreme chaos, she prayed for guidance-- for some form of hope--to pull her through her despair. She attempted to channel her chaos and find reason. Her hope and lasting touch with her daughter came in the form of an impossible phone call that could not have been made in the physical world.

EMBODY GRATITUDE

When we recount the stories of coincidence and miracle in our minds, there is one profound and unyielding emotion that determines the repeated occurrence of miracles in our lives: gratitude. When we ponder major positive life-changing events, the resounding emotion in your heart is gratitude. Gratitude will transform any emotion, no matter how dark or unmanageable it may seem. It is an elixir that heals sordid wounds and mends broken hearts. Our experience of gratitude is infinite, meaning once we experience it, the power of it never leaves us. Amazingly, the simple intention to experience it will attract more events that cause you to feel it. Gratitude is a magnifier. If we direct our energy toward it, all energies seem automatically enhanced as well.

Yet, when we focus on the "busi-ness" of life, we lose track of gratitude. We find ourselves focusing on the negative, such as a slow driver in front of us, instead of being grateful for the fact that it is a beautiful day and we have additional time to relax or plan during the car ride.

If you are not certain where to start with energy, I encourage you to start with gratitude. Gratitude is an easy energy to amplify. Play around with this energy. Express it when someone is least expecting it. Back your expression of it with energy and emotion. Often, we say thank you to the check-out clerk at the grocery. How many times a day do they get to say those words? Surprise them with a heart-felt communication.

The energy of gratitude has amplified my life to far exceed my imagination. I am grateful for my miracles:

I have healed my migraines; I am grateful for my health. I have found what I didn't know I was searching for in the church parking lot. I am grateful for my power. I cherish every day making memories with my husband, kids, and family; I am grateful for their laughter and love. I am energetic; I am grateful for the love of my teacher(s). I share my amazement and difficulties with friends and family, who are my perpetual sounding boards. I am grateful for their honesty and wisdom. I share my perspective of energy; I am grateful for you.

I am grateful for my mother, who has always, lovingly, edited every ineptly expressed idea I put to paper or in the computer. Her ability to help me transform and convey what is stuck in my head into written and logical form is truly miraculous. Without such "translating,", I would not be able to adequately share these stories and perspectives with you.

I am also grateful for my father, who was in a head-on-collision with a semi-truck a few years ago. Not only did he climb out of his vehicle (with shattered ribs, punctured organs and a decimated leg), but he managed to recover well enough to ski with his grandsons. I am most appreciative of his being granted more time with us, and greatly treasure a key strategy he taught me:

"Deal from strength, Kari. Figure out what your gifts are, and focus on those."

The energetic perspective is my strength. I invite you to join me and make it yours!

With infinite gratitude, thank you.

SUMMARY:

ATTRIBUTES OF MIRACLES:

Miracles occur when the probability collapses in an improbable manner.

Your energy body is the source that observes the environment and energies around you.

We are an integral part of the energetic dance around us.

Quantum particles take all paths; our observation is what collapses the path to the specific result.

PART THREE

Energy Positive Lifestyle: Guidelines and Supplemental Exercises

Kari Caldwell

Let the beauty of what you love be what you do.

—Rumi

ENERGY POSITIVE LIFESTYLE:
GUIDELINES

Understanding your world from an energetic perspective may seem like a daunting task. After all, your mind may still be grappling with the concept that everything and nothing can be occurring simultaneously! When I began to explore energy, I couldn't absorb enough information fast enough to help me understand what I was finding. The more changes I made, the more I felt myself getting "caught" by the idiosyncrasies that come with learning any new concept—it seemed I would take two steps ahead, but feel like I had taken three backwards. When you're trying to maintain very optimistic thoughts, and digest numerous new concepts and visualizations, it's easy to become frustrated and feel overwhelmed. At times I wanted a list of simple, non-negotiable guidelines to follow to help me make the frequent and tough decisions on my new path.

In my exploration I found that having such guidelines and boundaries do matter. In our culture today, there is a tendency to stretch boundaries, let people get away with lies, and not demand accountability for personal actions. In other words, the barrier between right and wrong has become blurred.

In the energy world, however, lines of positivity and negativity are not blurred. If you want to experience empowerment and an abundance of health, happiness, and love, you must set limits, follow guidelines, and release your old, outdated thought patterns. Once you achieve this, you will experience your intentions and feel success!

You may have picked up this book because you were curious or maybe because you want to know how to fix a particular problem. But, by now you recognize this book contains grand parameters for lifestyle change; not just a specific set of directions for a singular issue. You may no longer want to *only* solve a problem; you will want to experience a whole new perspective that is guided by rules and patterns. As you progress, you will become familiar with positive energy that is always there for you on a permanent basis. Following these simple, non-negotiable energy positive guidelines will ensure confidence and clarity in your pursuit of your dreams and intentions.

I wish I could tell you that once you adapt the Energy Positive Perspective, your life will be "easy." But the honest reality is that everyone has old, deep-seated energies and it can take time to learn how to transform and move your thoughts. You must learn to build unyielding, internal beliefs about your intentions and how to best support them.

In short, when in doubt, you can just follow the Energy Positive guidelines! You will find a brief review of these guidelines, and then see supplemental exercises to help you get organized and prepare for success!

Energy Positive Lifestyle: Guidelines

1. Choose different and new energies every day, including emotions and experiences in order to stop unfavorable patterns from repeating.

2. Choose your words and thoughts intentionally.

3. Have faith.

4. Give yourself permission.

5. Understand abundance.

6. Always look for the greatest and best outcome for everyone involved.

7. Know what you control. This includes the past and the future.

8. Let go of your need to control outcomes.

9. Take charge of your own energetic story. Establish boundaries and stick to them. Stop the outside energies that do not serve you from entering your energy field.

10. Supercharge everything with gratitude.

Energy Positive Lifestyle: Guidelines

11. Turn down the internal noise in your mind.

12. Understand that transformation requires baby steps—nothing will happen overnight.

13. Chose foods and emotions that support your energy body.

14. Forgive yourself and love the food you put into your body, whether healthy or not.

15. Depend on your intuition. Play with it. Trust it.

16. Check in with your energy at the level of your body, mind, and spirit.

17. Embody gratitude.

18. Seek out synchronicity, recognize it and be grateful for it.

19. Discern the significance of coincidence and miracles around you.

20. Expect the unexpected! Look for positive and welcome improbable outcomes.

Energy Positive Lifestyle:
Supplemental Exercises

Daily activities and suggestions designed to empower you to progressively make choices that enforce an Energy Positive+ state of being.

Kari Caldwell

Exercises for Strategy 1:

Change Your Choice, Reclaim Your Power

Purpose: Reclaim Your Power

CHOICE
Choose how you respond: Accept negativity and chaos as an opportunity. This openness to change facilitates the rapid flow of the negative energies and recognition of the purpose they are serving. When you choose a positive response, you change your relationship with the choices that affect you. Instead of experiencing devastation, you may experience a renewed sense of empowerment and strength.

Recognize the power that comes when we do not allow ourselves to be the victim. Other people readily make changes that they believe are in their own best interest, sometimes to our apparent detriment. You and you alone, can choose to honor their choice and recognize that by not "playing the victim," you are owning your personal power.

TYPES OF CHOICE:

Proactive Choice: When we choose to be proactive, we take control of the energy around us and can intentionally assert our energies where we choose, not where the energies "happen" to lead us.

Personal Choice: There are some choices that reflect situations that we do not control. When we accept circumstance beyond our control, we discover freedom of worry, doubt, and aggravation. You can choose your emotions, such as joy, happiness, or sorrow and worry.

Word Choice: What does your inner dialogue sound like? How many negative thoughts creep into your mind? Words are both our greatest asset and our "Achilles heel." A word will literally reproduce its exact energy. For example, if you think, "I will not get sick this year," you will attract the energy of "sickness," because, ironically, energy does not understand the negative "not." The proper use of words intended to attract health is, "I am healthful this year." When utilizing words, it is most critical to eliminate any "negative" word. In fact, the energy around you interprets your messages so literally that you can cancel the manifestation of even the best laid plans.

Exercises

CHOOSE DIFFERENT DAILY:

Choose an alternative route to work or school. While it may seem insignificant to change a route, a minor re-routing can open the door for dramatic new energies to enter your life.

Choose to feel beautiful. How often do you give yourself permission to look good? We get caught up in busy schedules and rarely commit to "looking good." Today, choose beauty.

Choose to do something that supports your health. Eat something fresh and healthful that you may skip otherwise. Choose to take the stairs.

Choose to not feel fear, anxiety or stress. Easier said than done. This choice, however, becomes easier the more we recognize what we actually control, as opposed to what exists in the future and has not occurred, and what exists in the past and is beyond our control. All events occur at their intended time.

Choose to be neutral. Let the drama pass you by. When we choose to disengage from drama, it is amazing how "quiet" and manageable our lives become. If you aren't certain if you should engage or not, ask yourself, "Do I really control the outcome of this situation?" or "Will all of my efforts influence their opinion?" When we choose to release other people's judgments, we take a neutral stance, and reclaim our power.

Choose to be bad. Treat yourself to a fun activity that you would normally not give yourself permission to choose. Grab an ice cream cone, leave work early, or sleep in longer than you should. Changing your routine and commitment to structure releases the energy of the structure around you.

LISTEN TO YOUR THOUGHTS AND WORDS:

While driving: Pay attention while you are driving or generally interacting with people. How irritated do you feel? Do other car drivers send you into a little road rage? Try to incorporate patience. What thoughts run through your head? Are you reviewing your day? Spending wasteful time gossiping on the phone?

When writing your intentions or releases, pay attention to your choice of words. Do not use any words that you no longer wish to experience. While writing this section, a fly kept buzzing my head. I kept thinking, "I wish this fly would go away." But the thought I was projecting was "Fly, Fly, Fly." As soon as I intentionally shifted my thought to, "Quiet and calm," the pesky fly disappeared.

While a fly in your face seems rather insignificant, the importance of good word choice is imperative when you write your releases and intentions. If you want to experience greater flow of money energy, you would write, "I experience an abundance of money energy," not, "I need more money."

ENERGY POSITIVE WRITING EXERCISE

Every time we translate a thought or word to the written page, we give the energy a physical reference point. While writing may seem insignificant in practice, it is critical to manifesting energy. For all writing exercises, you cannot repeat enough times what you put on paper. The more it goes on paper the more the intended energy builds around it.

A few suggestions: Pick any journal. Sometimes I like to choose notes with bright colors. Other times, I might use any old notebook that is laying around. I usually choose to write to my "energetic self," however, all of these decisions will be unique unto you!

One: Write your commitments.

Your choices are irrelevant without your commitment. Mean what you say, and say what you mean. Your commitment to your ideas, principles and intentions will ensure your confidence and faith in any and all decisions.

Two: Write out the choices that you can choose differently.

Once you identify your commitments, prioritize and question what is asked of you with each one. Where does your mind say yes and your heart say no or vice versa? Then develop a list of choices that you can begin to change.

Three: Don't be afraid to choose outside the box!

Choosing outside the box infuses a lot of new energy instantly. Even if you are only writing your "outside the box" choice, writing it strengthens the intended energy and releases the stronghold that patterns and established energy have over events in your life. If you choose to act on the "outside the box" choice, expect a huge "ripple effect" and be confident that if you are committed to your choice and intentions, everything will work out for the better.

Four: Recognize any patterns that shifted because you made a different choice.

Obviously if you choose outside the box, there will be a huge change in patterns! It is equally important to pay attention to the seemingly insignificant pattern changes also. Even if you take a different route to work and find out you avoided a traffic jam, pay attention. Give gratitude and write about it.

Exercises for Strategy 2:

Dream Big

Purpose: Expand your energy

INTENTIONS

Dreaming big is a great mechanism to get clear on your intentions. Imagining our dreams helps us to get organized, gather energy, resources, information and support for what we want to accomplish.

Exercises

THE CIRCLE OF LIFE

The Circle of Life ® from the Institute of Integrative Nutrition is a visual way to assess your alignment with your intentions. It helps you determine where your strengths and weaknesses lie, where you may need work, and where you may not be ready. The Circle of Life will help you discover new intentions and infuse new perspectives on old energies.

To complete the Circle of Life ®:

1) Ask yourself: What does success feel like in each area?

2) Place a dot at the center of the circle or close to the middle if you're dissatisfied with a particular category. Place a dot on the edge of the category if you are satisfied or happy.

3) If you have trouble completing it visually, you can always rank each category from 1-10. One represents the closest to the center and 10 is on the edge.

Little Book of Energy

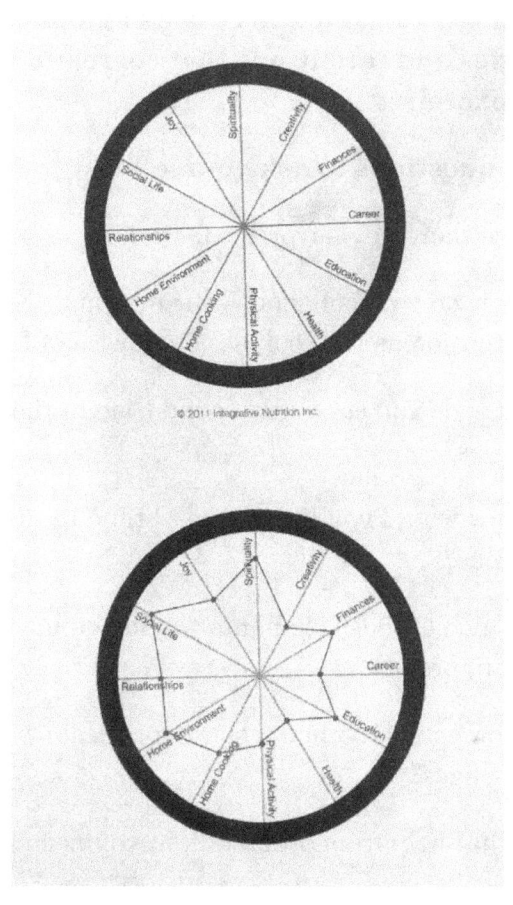

© 2011 Integrative Nutrition Inc.

The Circle of Life is an excellent tool to "get your intention-setting juices flowing." Although the circle focuses on physical aspects of your life, there are obvious energies and intentions that correlate with each exercise.

Some questions to ask yourself:

>Are there any surprises for you?

>How do you feel about your personal situation as you look at your Circle of Life?

>How do you currently spend time in those areas?

>How would you like to spend time in these areas?

>Which of these elements would you most like to improve?

>How could you make space for these changes?

>What help from others might you need?

>What would make it a better circle?

>What would a balanced circle look like to you?

ENERGY POSITIVE WRITING EXERCISE

Write, write, write! Explore your dreams and intentions on paper.

For dream work, I always write in a brightly colored journal (unless it is for a burn). Color incorporates energy and can help get your creative juices flowing!

VISION WORK

Most vision work focuses on creating a board or visual images of what you want to experience in your life. If you have had success with this exercise, then continue with it. Personally, I find vision boards to be too limiting for what I want to create. I like to focus on simply writing the energies I want to experience. For example, I may write, "I am happy," "I am focused," "I am love," "I am laughter," "I am finished with this book."

I find that allowing these energies to just flow without a lot of effort or thought or need to be "prepared" makes it much easier to repeat writing them daily.

Also notice the tense I used. Even though the book is not quite finished. If I were to write "I am finishing this book," the intention would be to continue to be "finishing," not actually complete.

Vision work in summary:

1) Write your intentions.

2) Write them as many times as you deem necessary. If new to working with energy, I recommend repeating the exercise daily for three weeks.

3) Be particular about your use of words and tense.

4) You can also incorporate them into your routine. For example, when I have a specific intention, I will put it in my phone as an appointment. I set an alarm for it so that the reminder "pops up." I still enjoy getting reminders from intentions I set several years ago. They serve as a great barometer for how far I have come, and where I want to continue to go.

DREAMS

Growth and expansion always starts with a seed that you cannot see on the outside. Thus the need for dreaming; we must create the seed.

Dreaming helps us channel our chaos; it sets the compass for how the energy around us can manifest. There are infinite possibilities existing simultaneously; our ability to be creative and imagine these possibilities determines the outcome of our experience.

In order to dream, we must be willing to really explore our boundaries—and then step beyond. We also must prioritize what we want to experience. Focusing on multiple dreams can cause distraction, delay and frustration.

As you contemplate your dreams consider the following:

When we prioritize we stay balanced. Our priorities help us direct where to focus on overloaded agendas and direction of our dreams.

Priorities aren't always what you think. Priorities can support emotions instead of practicality. In other words, if your heart tells you one thing, and your mind another, only your priorities will help direct your choices. For example, if you have a deadline, your mind will tell you to forge ahead, but your heart may suggest some much needed rest.

Emotional priorities are critical to listen to. When we avoid emotional priorities we are subject to triggering highly dramatic responses , which inevitably cause delay and unnecessary anxiety.

DISCOVER WHAT IS STOPPING YOU:

Figure out what will help you Dream Big. If it means you purchase lotto tickets, then by all means do it! We all have different limiting beliefs that prevent us from dreaming bigger than life. The key is to identify what holds you back and write out what you would do without that limitation in your way. Whatever you choose, paste a representation of it, e.g., your lotto tickets, with your dreams.

BURN(S)

The practice of burning a written dream or a prayer is symbolic of helping the thought or emotion transform from the physical into the spiritual. By physically watching your words release into the "ethers," you discover a unity and connection with the greater flow of energy around you. Conducting a "Burn" to seek new energy is best done in alignment with a new moon. New moons are symbolic of new beginnings; and, accordingly, they usher new energies into your life.

CREATIVITY

"Channel your Chaos. Exercising creativity means you become a master of chaos and destruction. All creative forces infuse the energies of chaos and destruction in order to transform the status quo and normal into the functional and beautiful."

If only we were all so competent in channeling our chaos!

In order to access the creative force required to channel chaos, we MUST practice being creative! As I've mentioned earlier in the book, I spent years in a corporate, linear, analytical mindset. Creativity was significantly lacking. Whether you are like me or you've never lost your creative spark, developing your creative energy is critical to expanding your ability to imagine and dream infinite possibilities.

Creativity is unique to each individual who expresses it. But it is critical to consciously draw your attention to the need for it.

For the "beginner" go to a craft store and try a new endeavor that incorporates some use of color. Pick any color you are drawn to and work it into your practice.

If that seems uninteresting, find a local pottery shop and spend an afternoon creating a piece of art.

I've found that it is much easier to be creative, when we know there is a greater purpose for it.

Think outside of the box. Creativity and risk always expand your energetic container.

LISTEN TO MUSIC, DO A CRAFT, PAINT, DOODLE, TAKE PICUTRES.

Exercises for Strategy 3:

Own Your Story: Own Your Power

Purpose: Release Energy

RELEASE

Releasing empowers us to own our story by moving stagnant energy and patterns of thought and behavior that no longer serve us. We collect experiences and energies throughout our lives. They fill our energetic "container" until the point it seems full. Releasing allows us to move the less favorable energies out before any good energy spills "over the dam." This proactive effort to control our energy empowers us to transform-- instead of being transformed--by the negative energies.

As you evaluate your story, you will begin to recognize your expectations and judgments, especially around relationships with yourself and others.

TYPES OF RELEASES

Positive energy for impending or long term goal

Psychological: how you hold fear, worry and anxiety

Emotional: stress, worry and anxiety

Limiting beliefs that deny us support

Toxins in the body

Regret and disappointments

Other people's insanity and drama

Attachments to old dreams and expectations

Structure and form around projects, partnerships, and finances. If they dissolve, energy is released and made available for better use. If projects move forward, support them intentionally.

RESULT of RELEASE:

Freedom of judgment and expectation

Space and opportunity for new energy

Magnification of abundant, supportive energies

Purification as a natural cleansing of accumulated negative energies

Ease and grace

Exercises

QUIET THE NOISE

Critical thinking blocks the knowledge of what we are looking for and what we are ready to release. When we don't know what's ahead, we become overwhelmed by too many choices.

If you are struggling to write or identify what you want to "get rid of," I recommend you start writing anything in your head. If you are constantly distracted by you grocery list, write it out. If you are distracted by a disagreement you had earlier in the day, then write about it.

Giving ourselves permission to write absolutely anything, gives our mind permission to continue to do its all-important job of analyzing and evaluating. This means that your mind will most likely kick into overdrive if you try to access difficult emotions and feelings around topics you no longer wish to experience. Until your mind becomes accustomed to letting your heart do the writing, just put down simple thoughts. Often, I'll catch my mind doing a side dialogue. I could be writing about a particular negative emotion, and I will hear "in the back of my mind" something like, "idiot, you should have known better." I patiently observe these thoughts and dismiss them. In this case, my mind is simply giving me more "judgments" to release!

BURN(S)

Conducting a "Burn" to release energy is best done in alignment with a full moon. Full moons carry cleansing and transformational energies with them.

CLEANSE

Focusing on health and well-being and cleansing toxins from your body are intense means to begin to transform energy. When clients are seeking to "jump start" their journey, I will often recommend a cleanse with food.

Our body is a barometer for the energies we are experiencing. Choosing to cleanse will "trigger" the release of physical toxins. When physical toxins flow out, energetic toxins follow.

As a Certified Health Coach through the Institute of Integrative Nutrition, I learned that every individual is physiologically different and therefore has different preferences and needs. Some people like to choose extreme cleanses, while others like to refrain from eating a certain food (e.g., giving up sugar or coffee).

Personally, I follow an elimination diet protocol. I find that a simple two-week process of changing sensitivity foods is easy to manage, and puts the focus on eating or taking in, as opposed to focusing on deprivation. This approach creates sustainable transition for the long-term.

Choose what is right for you. However, if you need help identifying solutions, you may find more information at www.energypositivelife.com.

EXERCISING:

When you exercise with the intention of engaging your center energy, you move your body physically forward; as you cause your cells to regenerate, and the energy around you loosens and releases. Think of having a good workout. Usually, we describe it as a great way to "clear our mind." We experience the mind clearing because typically when we exercise we have cleared our energy. Accordingly, once we've cleared our energy, our mind has less information to process.

Exercises for Strategy 4:

Fuel Your Energy Body

Purpose: Expand your Energy

THE DETAILS CREATE GRATITUDE

Every day we choose to fuel our bodies. Focus on this nurturing energy that already exists in your life. Attaching intention to your daily activities creates a greater awareness and flow of positive supportive energies. As a result, you add greater significance and meaning, and begin to feel a deep appreciation for the care you are providing your body.

Exercises

PRACTICE BALANCE

Creating balance in all aspects of your life is an easy and powerful way to promote the flow of energy. Here are some suggestions for areas to balance:

Complete one activity before moving onto another.

Disengage temporarily from relationships stuck in old patterns or that throw you out of balance. If you can handle re-engaging with your new boundaries in place, then do so. Otherwise, recognize that the relationship no longer supports your energy.

Balance your environment by focusing on how you are supported rather than on apparent interferences.

Balance your hormones, digestive system and weight. Our food and stress play a pivotal role in supporting these energies. Instead of jumping for a medication, try balancing your foods.

Balance workplace and finance.

Balance your heart and its focus of attention.

Balance work responsibilities.

DAILY ACTIVITES TO CREATE BALANCE:

Food Choice:

Working with your food choice is a powerful means to attracting the energy of change into your life—and a very accessible activity.

Bio-Individuality ®.The most important thing you can do when it comes to food choice is to recognize what works for you and stick with it:

> *Recognize your bio-individuality. No perfect way of eating works for everybody. The food that is perfect for your unique body, age and lifestyle may make another person gain weight and feel lethargic. Similarly, no perfect way of eating will work for you all the time. You may notice you eat different foods or days when you are working eight hours than on a relaxing day spent reading. Foods you ate as a child may not agree with you as an adult. What you crave in the winter is completely different than what you crave in the summer.* (Rosenthal, Integrative Nutrition: feed your hunger for health and happiness, 2007, 2011, 2014)

If you aren't certain what works, try an elimination diet. In my personal experience and working with clients, I've found that the elimination diet is the easiest way to discover food sensitivities (foods that may be causing low-level inflammation or negative reactions).

Create Balance. Once you do identify the right food groups, stick with a 90/10 plan—especially if you are seeking weight loss. This means that 90% of the time you eat what works and 10% of the time you have flexibility to consume what you are craving.

Eat Clean and Green:

Incorporate greens into your food choices. Greens provide much needed nutrients and fiber to help your body process and digest both stress and foods. Greens help us eliminate toxins from our body. Intentionally releasing physical toxins promotes the release of energetic toxins as well.

Clean eating means eliminating processed foods. If you cannot pronounce the word on the label, chances are your body will not recognize what to do with the molecules in it either. The harder your body has to work to process food, the more your resources get diverted to the act of digestion. When the digestive system is taxed, and struggles to eliminate "molecules of food it does not recognize" or toxins, we may incur inflammation and stress. Often the skin as well is affected, and it should not have to need to aid in the ridding of junk in your gut!

Self-Care:

Often we don't focus enough on self-care. Self-care is one of the easiest activities to engage in to support your intentions. For example, hopefully you managed to brush your teeth today. Give yourself credit! Every little detail counts.

Recognize the self-care as a form of love. And set the intention to experience more opportunities for self-care and love.

Self-care can also include your energy body. Energy is "sticky." When we are in public, we often "pick-up" other people's energies. While you may not consciously recognize that you are carrying around other people's energy, you can relate to the feeling of it. Think of a time when you have been around someone who was "disgusting", most likely you felt like you needed to take a shower or exercise to "shake the feeling." This is your conscious mind receiving the message from your energy body or spirit that it needs a cleanse. Good energy hygiene requires cleaning "sticky" energies among other activities. Energy is easy to clean and can be achieved by simply imagining the sticky energies being cleared away. You can also pretend to utilize magnets to pull the sticky energies away from you.

Meditation:

The benefits of meditation have been directly linked to stress reduction. But the most beneficial aspect of meditation is that it facilitates our ability to do an energy inventory. Once we quiet our minds, the energies that need attention and seek to be transformed are what present themselves to us. Most of us think a meditation is a time-consuming process. And yes, in an ideal world everyone should spend far more time meditating than they actually do. But if you don't have time, ten minutes a day, spent quieting your mind, is a good start. If you are not certain how to meditate, you can check out www.energypositivelife.com for great starter meditations.

Emotion: "Get a grip"!

Whether you consider yourself to be an emotional person or not, we all experience varying degrees of different emotions—and that is a good thing! Often we think we are subject to our emotions or controlled by them. But when we choose to simply observe our own personal flow of emotions, we are able to appreciate the greater purpose they serve. Emotions not only direct and help coordinate the body, they are the energetic link between our physical and energy bodies. We can direct our attention to this connection to understand the cause of the emotion. Positive emotions indicate a connection with our intentions, while negative emotions indicate misalignment with our intentions. Therefore, focusing on the experience of positive emotion is a direct link to building expansive energies.

Emotions are like a roadmap for where energy needs to transform in our bodies.

Emotions are a part of us because they flow and move, but also they are like physical objects that can be moved, released, shaped and molded. Thinking of emotions in a physical context helps us detach from the physical experience of the emotion so that we may transform it. Consider the emotion of fear and sadness. Most likely, this quick thought made your chest get tight, or you experienced some form of constriction, somewhere in your body. Picture where the fear or sadness is in your body. Now imagine wrapping that part of your body in a golden bandage, like wrapping a present, and hold that part of your body with your hands. The physicality of the emotion transforms, and tension releases. Although this is a brief example, the theory applies universally to emotions and our body. Essentially, by imagining an emotion in a physical form and imaging doing physical things to it, we can help transform and heal the trauma around the part of the body where that emotion lives.

Positive Thoughts:

Point the energetic compass. Thinking positive thoughts is about so much more than just "maintaining a positive perspective." Humans literally *consume* our own thoughts. Typically, those thoughts also have emotions (with either a positive or negative charge) that gets consumed also. Depending on the composition of thought "charges" within our body (down to a cellular level), we determine the overall "charge" or signal that we broadcast into our environment. In other words, depending on the overall charge, we attract similar charges into our energy field. This overall signal, though, isn't fixed. It is dynamic and consists of every experience, thought and emotion. You won't experience them all at once. But events and circumstances that are in alignment with a certain charge will be attracted to that charge in your body.

Your brain's primary objective is *survival*. This means that depending on the variety of input, you mind will be drawn to whichever outcome seems the safest. And your body's interpretation of the safest outcome depends on the quantity and quality of filtered signals that get to the brain first. At any given time, a thought is simply your body's "best guess" out of a multitude of options.

Love is a good example. Many people speak about knowing a particular choice of partner is not good for them. Nevertheless, they will follow their heart. This is because the energy of love is very powerful. And for the mind to choose to break the "love" energy feels akin to death. So it will create as many scenarios and reasons as possible to ensure that short term survival occurs.

When we are subject to linear thought patterns (A>B>C), we become very fixed on the outcome, not the process. We think we will "lose love" permanently or not conceive. But, when we tell our mind we are committed to the interconnected (SPIDER) pattern, it factors that into the options. The mind is then tasked with the responsibility of co-creation instead of survival. This is a far more expansive tool to incorporate.

Exercise:

Exercise and energy have many obvious correlations, like building muscle and building positive energy. If you exercise, you obviously are sending a positive "regenerative" message to your body. What is most critical to recognize about exercise, however, is the need for a variety of types of exercise. Experiencing energy requires movement and flow throughout the body. I work with plenty of athletes who are exceptionally fit but are not limber and loose, so the energy in their bodies is not flexible. Yoga and Pilates are both excellent activities to balance with exercise to promote the flow of energy in your body.

If time constraints are an issue with exercise, be intentional about any and all physical activity. Even if for ten minutes, walk around the block or your backyard. Stretch. Do something.

Lastly, spending time outdoors infuses amazing natural energy into your body. When we exercise outdoors, we breathe deep and force fresh oxygen into more stagnant energy centers. Additionally, our energy body, including the aura, will naturally cleanse and release any negative energies, which is also referred to as "grounding."

Grounding:

"Grounding" is the energetic effect of connecting us to the natural energies of the earth. We experience these natural energies regularly. The most identifiable way to "feel" them is to think of how you feel after a walk on the beach, in the woods, or even in grass. We experience sensations of calmness and being supported and relaxed when we are grounded. Conversely, if you think of someone who is "flighty" or "ditsy," often their energy is not grounded.

Breathing:

Deep breathing is the most powerful tool you have to turn off your flight or fight response. The practice of deep breathing calms your nervous system and sends the message to your body to resume "regeneration." Deep breathing also facilitates the flow of energy throughout the body, especially when we take time to engage our abdomen in our breath.

Kari Caldwell

Exercises for Strategy 5:
Practice, Practice, Practice

PURPOSE: BUILD YOUR ENERGY ASSETS AND ACHIEVE BALANCE

STRIKE A BALANCE

The goal of Practice, Practice, Practice is to sufficiently build positive energies. This means we must strike a balance between sensing both positive and negative energies.

This balance comes with listening and observing. Intuition is the best tool we have for making this observation.

INTUITION

Intuition is our ability to know from a feeling, rather than utilizing conscious reasoning. Utilizing intuition requires learning to trust what you feel and sense what is right or true in order to guide you in the right direction.

Intuition will lead you to signs and confirmation that you are on the right path. All doors open and close when the timing is right. The energy around you will provide messages and insights that help you transition through these changes. Intuition will help you ascertain signs that are only recognizable when one door closes--and another door opens--revealing the possibilities of new opportunities.

Exercises

QUIET THE NOISE

Before we jump into meditation, I want to readdress quieting the mind. Critical thinking blocks the experience of connection. It was not until I worked with a meditation coach that I began to appreciate just how "noisy" my mind had been while meditating on my own.

Our mind's job is to make noise, evaluate and analyze situations. When we ask it to be quiet we are asking it to take a back seat and stop working. Quiet time is a counterintuitive exercise for the mind unless sleep is involved. When I first began meditating it would take so much effort to quiet my mind that I would fall asleep for the best parts of the meditation!

To quiet your mind:

1) Write every and anything down prior to meditation. This "empties" your mind.

2) Dialogue with your mind. Invite it to be a silent observer and to co-create solutions to problems it wants to solve in the middle of the meditation.

3) Inform your mind that it will receive an infinite number of new ideas and a keen "awareness" to play with when finished.

MEDITATION

When we meditate we access our inner energy and get a glimpse of an all-knowing, loving peace and contentment.

Meditation empowers us to identify and connect with our intentions. We can see what we are looking for in our heart rather than just in our mind.

In addition to utilizing meditation to quiet the mind, I love to identify peace and calm, and also visualize the energies within and develop tools and strategies to move them around. In other words, when we meditate we can identify what is blocking a certain intention by exploring how other energies resonate and conflict within our body. We can utilize energetic tools to help transform all of our energies within.

With this approach we can work directly with emotions without needing to experience the physical words and stories that typically accompany them. We can also direct support and regenerative energies to areas of the body that need healing. Whether experienced or not at meditating, I recommend working with a coach to recognize the full benefits of meditation. Anytime we look to acquire a new skill or increase our proficiency, we generally work with someone to learn the practice. Meditation is no different. Coaches guide you specifically through the energies that are present and push you to reach new levels of awareness. For more information on meditation coaching and meditations, please visit: www.energypositivelife.com.

In the meantime, I invite you to explore your own energetic body through meditation.

1) Quiet your mind.

2) Practice some deep breathing.

3) Feel your body relax into the floor.

4) Feel your muscles relax into your body and the tension around you melt away.

5) Then slowly begin to scan your body. Listen for what is speaking loudest. Maybe a part of your body is sore. Why is this? Is there a message or awareness your body needs you to recognize?

6) Explore any emotions or ideas that present themselves.

7) Most important, don't question or doubt what comes to you during your quiet time. Ideas can seem bizarre or random. Let the thoughts and memories come forward. You are breathing life into a new form of messaging.

INTUITION BUILDERS

Building your intuition can be a very literal practice. Applied Kinesiology and muscle testing are measures to determine the flow of energy through the body. This flow signifies when your intuition is engaged and when it is not. While the practice of learning muscle testing is more involved than the conversation allows in this book, there are a few great exercises you can learn on your own.

Think about the all-too-familiar "gut feeling." It represents a resounding warning that you should probably stop or proceed with caution.

Learning to fine tune the "gut feeling" is a quick, reliable way to know what your instinct, or the energy, is telling you.

Yes/No:

1) Take a deep breath and ask yourself something you know to be false. For example I would think, "My name is Sally Smith."

2) On the exhale, notice where you "feel" the "no" answer.

3) Now repeat the same thing except say a truth. For example I would think, "My name is Kari Caldwell."

4) Repeat this exercise over and over. Change the true/false statements. Continue to identify where your body resonates the true or false response. You will recognize that most "nos" occur in your gut, while the "yeses" are generally around your sternum or higher.

Follow your gut:

Another fun exercise is to follow your gut. Once you've perfected your yes/no activity, take it on the road. Utilize your yes/no actions while walking, driving, running, or shopping.

1) When you approach an intersection, ask yourself which direction you should go.

2) Follow whichever path your "gut" tells you.

3) Watch for different signs or symbols along the way.

I can't begin to tell you how many traffic jams I have avoided and prime parking spots I have found doing this exercise.

The results are usually interesting and easy to follow because you have minimal emotional attachment to the outcome. Your ability to build your intuition with insignificant events will make you that much more confident when you need to rely on it with more important events.

COLOR YOUR WORLD

Color is a great representation of energy. Every color represents different healing energies.

What colors are showing up for you? When you find yourself attracted to a certain color, consciously choose to use it daily, such as on your clothes, in a favorite photo, or on your phone.

SILENCE:

When we practice silence we choose to avoid engagement with people or patterns not in alignment with our intentions. Choosing silence, instead of "triggering," arguing, fighting back, or telling stories, empowers us to connect with the energy, vibrations and intelligent forces. Stay neutral and see the situation as an expression of necessary evolution.

Practicing silence requires faith, trust and creativity to achieve the energies of discernment, patience and acceptance.

How to practice Silence:

Disengage: Practice neutrality in expectation and judgment with new and old connections.

Skip out on gossip: By participating in gossip, you divert your energy and power to events, people and circumstances over which you have no control. While gossip may seem beneficial or necessary, the long term effects of continually diminishing your power are substantial.

Hold your tongue. Easier said than done, right? Practicing silence when someone is picking a fight is challenging. But, maintaining distance is rewarding. When we choose to respond differently, we regain control and power over our emotions.

Exercises for Strategy 6:

Expect Miracles

Purpose: Receive positive energy, receive miracles

RECEIVE

Expecting miracles means that you expect to receive.

When you are a master of receiving, you ensure that both positive and negative energies are flowing.

When you are conditioned to giving, practicing receiving can be a grueling process. But with commitment, receiving becomes increasingly easier, and exceptionally rewarding!

Miracles often occur when improbable energy is present. Improbable energy rarely feels safe and often has a negative connotation. The better we get at receiving and managing improbability, the greater our chance of receiving miracles.

Exercises

PRACTICE RECEIVING

Practice asking for help where you normally wouldn't. Maybe when you can't locate items at the grocery store, ask for help.

Accept compliments gracefully.

Take time for yourself, whether eating and enjoying a meal or not rushing yourself in the shower. Really appreciate the time you have for yourself.

Accept an invitation from a friend for lunch.

Spend time outside. Enjoy the seasons. Begin to pay attention to the rhythms around you. What are the trees doing? Where is the moon in its cycle?

MITIGATE CHAOS

Chaos is improbable. Nobody wants to have to manage improbable energies, but when we get good at it, we stand a better chance of decreasing the cycle of negativity.

1) Stay grounded. This means connect with family, friends, nature, your roots. Do anything that helps you keep yourself focused in reality.

2) Do not think about the future or past. Just address what you control in the moment. This means you do not dwell on what could be, what should be, or what was.

3) Make certain that every choice is made with thought and intention to support your positive intentions.

4) Have faith and courage.

PRACTICE GRATITUDE

Focus on giving gratitude without being prompted or asked. When we give gratitude freely we intentionally move energy to create a reception of energy.

A powerful gratitude practice is to express gratitude for energies that are difficult. When we focus on the aspects of a relationship that we are grateful for, and express this gratitude, we diffuse the power our negative aspects hold over us. This diffusing of power gives us the ability to see the people or situation clearly.

To practice gratitude:

1) Connect with people who hold special significance in your life even if you have lost touch with them. Write a letter or place a call.

2) Write a gratitude list. Consider everything you are grateful for. You can even do a Burn for this list.

3) Choose positivity. Instead of thinking about a negative feature or attribute, find a positive one and be grateful for that.

4) Vow not to complain or criticize.

5) Give at least one compliment every day.

Heartfelt Appreciation

This book would not exist without all of the teachers and students who have come before me and shared their lessons. My special mention is to Shweta. Your gifts have given me courage and perspective to experience my life in a new light. You literally keep me grounded in my dreams. Thank you.

Without Julie's and Mary's honest opinions and strong motivation, I might not have stuck with my vision. Thank you!

To all of my family, your love and support empowers me to be an awesome mother, wife, friend, sister, and daughter.

To my husband and boys, for your continued patience, love and support.

And

To you, thank you for investing your trust and vision in the Little Book of Energy.

ABOUT THE AUTHOR

Kari Caldwell lives with her husband and three rambunctious boys. When she is not carting the kids around or overseeing homework, she transforms her own and other people's negative energies. And makes a profound difference in their lives with her intuitive coaching style. Known an enthusiastic and dynamic speaker, she is frequently engaged in sharing her energetic stories.

END NOTES

Page 44: Shenvi, Neil; Quantum Mechanics and Materialism (essay)

Page 48: Eden, Donna; Energy Medecine, Balancing the Body's Energies (2008)

Page 52: Eden, Donna; Energy Medecine, Balancing the Body's Energies (2008)

Page 53: Eden, Donna; Energy Medecine, Balancing the Body's Energies (2008)

Page 59: Weismann, Dr. Darren R.; The Power of Infinite Love and gratitude (1997)

Page 160: Weismann, Dr. Darren R.; The Power of Infinite Love and gratitude (1997)

Page 195: Tarnas, Richard; Cosmos and Psyche (2006)

Page 245: Rosenthal, Joshua; Integrative Nutrition (2007, 2001, 2014)

Kari Caldwell

Are you Energy Positive+?

Recognize Progressively Expansive Energies and learn more about Leveraging Negativity!

Visit www.energypositivelife.com for details.

www.ingramcontent.com/pod-product-compliance
Lightning Source LLC
LaVergne TN
LVHW051824080426
835512LV00018B/2723